THE BRITISH RAJ: KEYWORDS

For two hundred years India was the jewel in the British imperial crown. During the course of governing India – the Raj – a number of words came to have particular meanings in the imperial lexicon. This book documents the words and terms that the British used to describe, define, understand and judge the subcontinent. It offers insight into the cultures of the Raj through a sampling of its various terms, concepts and nomenclature, and utilizes critical commentaries on specific domains to illuminate not only the linguistic meaning of a word but its cultural and political nuances.

This fascinating book also provides literary and cultural texts from the colonial canon where these Anglo-Indian colloquialisms, terms and official jargon occurred. It enables us to glean a sense of the Empire's linguistic and cultural tensions, negotiations and adaptations. The work will interest students and researchers of history, language and literature, colonialism, cultural studies, imperialism and the British Raj, and South Asian studies.

Pramod K. Nayar teaches at the Department of English, University of Hyderabad, India. His most recent books include *The Indian Graphic Novel: Nation, History and Critique* (Routledge, 2016), *The Transnational in English Literature: Shakespeare to the Modern* (Routledge, 2015), the edited *Postcolonial Studies: An Anthology* (2015) and the *Postcolonial Studies Dictionary* (2015). A book on human rights and literature and an edited five-volume collection *Indian Travel Writing, 1830–1947* (Routledge) are forthcoming.

THE BRITISH RAJ: KEYWORDS

Pramod K. Nayar

LONDON AND NEW YORK

First published 2017
by Routledge
2 Park Square, Milton Park, Abingdon, Oxon OX14 4RN

and by Routledge
711 Third Avenue, New York, NY 10017

*Routledge is an imprint of the Taylor & Francis Group,
an informa business*

© 2017 Pramod K. Nayar

The right of Pramod K. Nayar to be identified as author of this work has been asserted by him in accordance with sections 77 and 78 of the Copyright, Designs and Patents Act 1988.

All rights reserved. No part of this book may be reprinted or reproduced or utilised in any form or by any electronic, mechanical, or other means, now known or hereafter invented, including photocopying and recording, or in any information storage or retrieval system, without permission in writing from the publishers.

Trademark notice: Product or corporate names may be trademarks or registered trademarks, and are used only for identification and explanation without intent to infringe.

British Library Cataloguing-in-Publication Data
A catalogue record for this book is available from the British Library

Library of Congress Cataloging-in-Publication Data
A catalog record has been requested for this book

ISBN: 978-1-138-28009-0 (hbk)
ISBN: 978-1-315-26722-7 (ebk)

Typeset in Sabon
by Apex CoVantage, LLC

CONTENTS

Preface	vi
Acknowledgements	vii
Introduction	1
Keywords	19
Bibliography	155

PREFACE

The British Raj: Keywords is a prospect view than an on-the-ground full survey. As such, it offers a panoramic view of the Raj. But the devil, as we know, is in the details. These details may be found in the primary texts that are cited through the entries.

The entries have been selected for their cultural significance in British India, and for their curiosity value. Evidence from texts are, as far as possible, entertaining and informative for the entry concerned.

Place names have been left out although this has meant sacrificing institutions like Haileybury and the Asiatic Society or the number of organizations that constitute the social, literary and cultural landscape of British India.

ACKNOWLEDGEMENTS

It is a pleasure to acknowledge, for varied acts of encouragement, teaching, stimulation, kindness, love, tolerance, support and critical inputs:

My parents and parents-in-law;
Nandini and Pranav;
Mohan Ramanan and Sudhakar Marathe;
Ajeet, Ibrahim, Neelu, Molly, Josy, Ron, Premlata, Walter;
Nandana;
The Works of P.G. Wodehouse;
K. Narayana Chandran *and*
Anna Kurian.

I acknowledge with special gratitude the reviewers of the proposal and early draft for suggestions and comments.

Thanks to Shoma Choudhury of Routledge India for her sustained enthusiasm at the project, but with apologies for not doing the book *she* wanted!

INTRODUCTION

What varied opinions we constantly hear
Of our rich Oriental possessions;
What a jumble of notions, distorted and queer,
Form an Englishman's "Indian impressions!"

First a sun, fierce and glaring, that scorches and bakes
Palankeens, perspiration, and worry;
Mosquitoes, thugs, cocoa-nuts, Brahmins, and snakes,
With elephants, tigers, and Curry.

Then Juggernaut, punkahs, tanks, buffaloes, forts,
With bangles, mosques, nautches, and dhingees;
A mixture of temples, Mahometans, ghats,
With scorpions, Hindoos, and Feringhees.

Then jungles, fakeers, dancing-girls, prickly heat,
Shawls, idols, durbars, brandy-pawny;
Rupees, clever jugglers, dust-storms, slipper'd feet,
Rainy season, and mulligatawny.

Hot winds, holy monkeys, tall minarets, Rice,
With crocodiles, ryots or farmers;
Himalayas, fat baboos, with paunches and pice,
So airily clad in pyjamas.

With Rajahs – But stop, I must really desist,
And let each one enjoy his opinions,
Whilst I show in what style Anglo-Indians exist
In her Majesty's Eastern dominions.
　　　　　　　　– Prefatory poem to G.F. Atkinson,
　　　　　　　　Curry and Rice on Forty Plates;
　　　　　　　　Or, The Ingredients of Social Life
　　　　　　　　at "Our Station" in India (1859)

INTRODUCTION

The above poem might very well be read as a synoptic introduction to the Raj, especially in its cultural manifestations and negotiations with the colonized culture. It also offers an inventory of the *terms* and *names* a reader is most likely to encounter when perusing any historical account, travelogue, administrative tract or literary text, right from the period of early settlements of the English in 'factories' in Surat in the seventeenth century to the establishment of the British political power in the Indian subcontinent towards the latter half of the eighteenth and the heyday of the Raj in the Victorian period. In one poem, Atkinson manages to summarize, describe, inventory and organize a vast variety of things Indian, and this poem-approaching-doggerel is symptomatic of the field we now recognize as colonial discourse. It instances an entire *lexicon* of imperial speech, description, writing and pronouncements.

Given the variety and numbers of bizarre, inexplicable, unexplainable and incomprehensible objects, practices and habits the British encountered in the subcontinent, their chief concern from the very first writings was to organize this material in a manageable way and in a language that administrators, businessmen, travelers, and the curious readers would understand. Colonial discourse, which took many forms, was a form of narrative and textual control over this uncontrollable and proliferating material. The discourse not only sought to explain the subcontinent, it also sought to construct it as a field of enquiry. The Indian peoples, practices and landscapes were objects to be *studied* and *commented* upon. If Atkinson's verse offers a witty catalogue, more encyclopedic works of reference like *Hobson-Jobson* – the amazing Anglo-Indian dictionary – embody a wholly different genre, but both contribute to the Empire's penchant for documentation, inventory and description.

This introduction to a volume that offers up the 'keywords' from the imperial lexicon is a quick tour of the enormous print and lexicographic empire of the British in India, an empire within which several generic engineering experiments and textual hybridization, such as Halhed's *Grammar* or Yule and Burnell's *Hobson-Jobson*, were performed. Rather than a political history of the Empire, it sets out to map this print landscape and its topography.

The printextual public sphere

A process of imperial editorial control, inquiry, studies and commentary required, given the amorphous, diverse nature of the material it was

INTRODUCTION

dealing with, many genres and modes of narration. It is this set of texts that constituted the 'imperial archive' upon which administrators, statesmen, reformers, mercenaries, priests, physicians, educators and military officers relied upon as they set about ruling the subcontinent. In Thomas Richards's words, the 'administrative core of the Empire was built around knowledge-producing institutions like the British Museum, the Royal Geographic Society, the India Survey, and the universities' (4). Each of these institutions compiled data and information in the form of printed matter on various topics immediate to their own professional requirements and interests. Following the tone set by Edward Said and Thomas Richards, among others, Miles Ogborn in *Indian Ink* (2007) demonstrated the scriptorial foundations of the British Empire in India. Print, Ogborn argues, was central to the way the British thought about, organized, dominated and engaged with their vast colony. Ogborn makes a case for a 'restricted public sphere of collective decision making' (76) with the rise of consultation books in the latter half of the seventeenth century. In similar fashion, account books, for Ogborn, became an index of the social and moral order of the factory itself (83). In this 'restricted public sphere' of early colonial print productions (1620–1800) about India one may identify the following genres: diaries, consultation books, accounts, grammars, histories, memorials, reflections, regulations, discourses, almanacs, 'true relations', letter books, annals, handbooks (*Vade mecum*), considerations, despatches and correspondence. From the nineteenth century, we come across reports from the Archaeological Society of India, cookery and housekeeping manuals, gardening advice books, conservation tracts, missionary narratives, hunting memoirs, botanists, zoological surveys, which also contributed to the East India Company (EIC) and British government debates. Many of these reports were cited in the House of Commons and Lords debates, as should be clear from even a rudimentary glance through the Parliamentary Papers on any India topic. These genres and forms, it must be noted, were not hermetically sealed textual spheres.

'Annals' such as the *Early Annals* (1895, compiling extracts from the *Bengal Public Consultations* of 1660–1748) offered the chronological framework for Indian and British events. 'Discourses' such as Thomas Mun's *A Discourse of Trade* (1621) offered justifications of policy. 'Reflections' and 'Considerations', such as the Dutchman William Bolts's *Considerations on Indian Affairs* (1772), were incorporated into English discourses due to British responses to them (Verelst's response to Bolts 1772) and stirred up debates and/or levelled charges of mismanagement against the EIC. Accounts such as J.Z. Holwell's *Genuine Narrative of the Deplorable Deaths of the English Gentlemen . . . in the Black Hole* (1758) offered personalized narratives of suffering. 'Regulations' were often drafted by the British Parliament for the 'Government of the British Territories in India and the Better Administration of Justice within the Same' as one such document was titled. The 'Almanac' was a detailed account of weather and climatic conditions, localized (such as the *Bengal Almanac*), recording phases of the moon but also offering ranks of the English officialdom in India, weights and measures and trader accounts. 'Grammars' were attempts to develop codified rules about Indian languages for the British officials in India, but also, as commentators have shown, contributed to the classification of Indian languages (Mir 2010 for Punjabi, for example). 'Histories', such as Robert Orme's *Historical Fragments of the Mogul Empire* (1782), constructed a narrative that sought to impose a linearity and order on Indian history for consumption by the English back home.

The public sphere generated by such vast amounts of print matter about the subcontinent was a 'restricted public sphere', as Ogborn calls it, because it was a textual public sphere. The textual public sphere in colonial India was a *print* response to and appropriation of an already-existing 'Indian ecumene', which C.A. Bayly in *Empire and Information* identified as a public sphere of debate worked through oral and scribal mode of communication (45). In other words, even *before* the print technology that was to transform India, oral and scribal forms of exchanges, letter writing, newsletters and discussions at *chowrahas* or places of worship had put in place a public sphere. There existed a huge world of writing and reading in native languages even before print (see Anindita Ghosh for Bengal 2006). On the other hand, the British instituted a public sphere of *English* in India founded on print and textual production, a printextual public sphere. This printextual public sphere, even if restricted as Ogborn seems to presume, is one that co-opts an Indian one in another significant way. The printextual public sphere of the first century of colonial India 'put into print narrative' meanings, texts, codes and information appropriated from the *munshis*, the native informants such as pundits and *maulvis* and translators. This is the case with the genres of maps and surveys, archaeological tracts, commentaries, grammars and reformist legislation.

Kavali Venkata Boriah contributed to Colin Mackenzie's archaeological documenting of the inscriptions of South Indian temples such as Mahabalipuram. In the case of Colin Mackenzie, Boriah and other Indian assistants drew maps and figures so that these became a part of the imperial archive. Mackenzie had about 17 translators, in addition to draftsmen, surveyors and copyists, according to one study (Howes 2009). Francis Wilford relied on native translators when crafting his geographical texts for India. Nigel Leask (2000) has commented on Francis Wilford's unnamed pundit, who provides him with the sources for a 'Hindu geography' (which appeared in the *Asiatick Researches* from 1799), and noted how Wilford also speaks of a group of brahmins who supported his claims. In the case of James Rennell, cartographer of Empire in the 1780s in works like *Memoir of a Map of Hindoostan* (1788) and Francis Buchanan in *A Journey from Madras through the Countries of Mysore, Canara and Malabar* (1807), very often the English surveyor relied on native informants. In fact, James Rennell appropriated the Mughal divisions of *subahs* into his work because 'the ideas of the boundaries are . . . impressed upon the minds of the natives by tradition' (1788: iii–iv). Such boundaries were not available for the Deccan region and so Rennell hoped to locate the 'modern divisions' there (iv). The map-makers, notes Matthew Edney (1997), 'even on those unavoidable occasions when observations patently failed and the indigenous informant had to be acknowledged, that information could still be absorbed into the British archive of factual, observed data' (81). Buchanan in fact relied upon 'proxy vision' and thus fitted into the 'established British practice of employing Indian artists to record natural and social scenes' (Edney 81). Halhed's *Grammar of the Bengal Language* (1788) required Bengali copyists to first copy from manuscript sources and then alphabets made before the type could be set. In each case we see the printextual public sphere constituted through a process by which common or specialized knowledge of the Indian public sphere entered the grammars, commentaries, research tracts and other genres of the printextual public sphere of the EIC.

In the case of social reform, especially in the early nineteenth century, a *consultative* process – and this is my third argument – clearly shaped the printextual public sphere. In the case of infanticide and *sati*, the British government in India treaded particularly carefully, anticipating native opposition, embarked on a process of consultation and deliberations with Indians. In the case of infanticide, for instance, the documents presented to the British parliament included transcripts of consultation with the native pundits, clan heads, the *taluqdars,* and others. For the purposes of evolving a clear set of legal doctrines and resolutions on these incendiary subjects, the British felt it would be wise to involve native 'experts' in the consultation. Many of these documents, such as John Cormack's *Account of Female Infanticide in Guzerat* (1815), reprinted the native comments and responses from Fatteh Mahomed, Sunderjee and others to questionnaires regarding the religious and scriptural foundations of the cultural practices of infanticide. Former officers of the Mughal Empire were called upon to offer their opinions regarding these rituals, opinions that were then incorporated into the colonial documentation and campaign against infanticide. Thus Mirza Mortiza's account of the Jarejha community in which he claimed that families wherein daughters were 'reared to maturity' and forced to find a groom later, were held 'in the greatest contempt' makes its way into the 'authoritative' document about infanticide (*Parliamentary Papers*, No. 426, 1824). A kind of court-hearing was held to examine native pundits on the history and theological-religious bases for the practice. In the case of *sati,* pundits were asked questions such as the following:

> In the event of a woman declaring her intention to burn with the body of her husband, and afterwards receding from such declaration, what would be the consequence, and what treatment would she experience from her relations?
> (*Parliamentary Papers*, No. 749, 1821)

The English public sphere also, as might be gathered, was being fashioned around India debates, manifest in publications such as the *Parliamentary Papers*.

Such examples instantiate the three-level argument I have been making: the print culture that constituted the public sphere mapped by Ogborn was not produced by the British surveyors, statesmen and soldier. It was a cross-over public sphere, a printextual one, *co-produced* by the British and their native cohorts of informants and commentators. This public sphere appropriated oral, scribal, folk texts and translations into an English print medium which then became the backbone of the colonial archive. It was made up of the consultations with native scholars and teachers that then found their way into public documents. Whether this printextual public sphere transcribed oral information received from indigenous informants and sources faithfully or manipulated it to suit their purpose we may never be able to affirm or reject with any degree of certainty. What is however certain is that the print making of the EIC's public sphere was always a crossover cultural space, even if it eventually came to embody the imperial archive as an instrument of domination.

Within this printextual public sphere, many genres co-existed.

INTRODUCTION

Generic engineering

The Inquiry as a proto-colonial narrative form flourished from the 1660s but has its roots in a genre that might be called 'Instructions'. Instructions for travellers were issued by various people from as early as the late sixteenth century. *Certain Briefe, and Special Instructions for Gentlemen, Merchants, Students, Soldiers, Mariners, and Others Employed in Services Abroad*, published in 1589, asked the traveller to organize the observations into sections such as cosmography, astronomy, geography, chorography, topography, husbandry, navigation, the political state, ecclesiastical state, literature, and histories and chronicles. Francis Bacon in his 1625 work, 'Of Travel', wrote:

> The things to be seen and observed are: the courts of princes, especially when they give audience to ambassadors; the courts of justice, while they sit and hear causes; and so of consistories ecclesiastic; the churches and monasteries, with the monuments which are therein extant; the walls and fortifications of cities, and towns, and so the heavens and harbors; antiquities and ruins; libraries; colleges, disputations, and lectures, where any are; shipping and navies; houses and gardens of state and pleasure, near great cities; armories; arsenals; magazines; exchanges; burses; warehouses; exercises of horsemanship, fencing, training of soldiers, and the like; comedies, such whereunto the better sort of persons do resort; treasuries of jewels and robes; cabinets and rarities; and, to conclude, whatsoever is memorable, in the places where they go.

The earl of Essex, Philip Sidney, and William Davison published *Profitable Instructions* in 1633. Robert Boyle compiled 'Inquiries for Surat', which were published in the *Philosophical Transactions of the Royal Society* (Vol. 2, No. 23 [1666–67]: 415–19). The philosopher John Locke also prepared a list of inquiries to François Bernier, the French physician-traveller (Daniel Carey 1996: 264). When Charles Cudworth was to depart for India, Locke sent him a letter with such inquiries:

> I would very gladly know whether . . . they [Indians] have any apparitions amongst them and what thoughts of spirits, and as

much of the opinions religion and ceremonys of the Hindoos and other heathens of those country . . . I should trouble you also with enquirys concerning their languages learning government manners and particularly Auranga-Zebe the Emperor of Indostan.

(Cited in Carey 1996: 264)

It is this Inquiry genre that animates *A Collection of Letters for the Improvement of Husbandry & Trade*, a periodical created by John Houghton, in the 1680s. Houghton's *Collection* was intended

For the advantage of tenant, landlord, corn-merchant, mealman, baker, brewer, feeder of cattle, farmer, maulster, grazier, seller and buyer of coals, hop-merchant, soap-boiler, tallow-chandler, wool-merchant, and their customers, & c . . . it was designed to give weekly from hence an account of the value of actions of the East-India, Guinea, Hudsons Bay, Linnen and Paper companies.

(cited in Ogborn 173)

Ogborn points out that the format of Houghton's *Collection*, with stock values and agricultural prices listed, was situated in a 'particular culture of information, knowledge and fact' (176) and continued the 'histories of the trades . . . taken up by the Royal Society and in particular by Robert Hooke, Robert Boyle, William Petty and John Evelyn' (178).

My point here is, within this culture of information-gathering and knowledge-making, we might discern the genealogy and hybridization of the *genres* that constituted these histories and even English prose styles. If the trader-reader demanded the inventory and catalogue of prices, the 'curious' scientific gentleman of the Royal Society sought a well-organized account of weather patterns. As I have proposed elsewhere, the Inquiry called for a catalogue of other cultures, from geography to architecture and poetry, even though their own theological, moral, mercantile financial, and other considerations undergirded the 'inquiries' (Nayar 2012: 32). Knowledge had to be organized in a form that would appeal to the range of readers Houghton lists above. What we see in the Inquiry and the Collection for prospective merchants in England is the hybridized account book, the ledger and the catalogue. The evolution of these hybrid genres testifies to the readership and hence the printextual public sphere that helped organize the subcontinent into a comprehensible entity preliminary to governance. The Inquiry, the Collection and the Account are *functional equivalents* even if they exhibit differences among themselves. These also anticipate the various 'Digests', of laws, missionary activities and such produced throughout the nineteenth century.

A 1608–09 bond executed by the pursers when they embarked on their voyage to India made it mandatory for them to maintain an inventory:

> of all such provisions tackle munitions furniture victuals and other necessaries which are or shall be during the said voyage brought aboard the said ship . . . also an inventory of all the goods, wares and merchandise as shall be brought into or carried of [sic] the said ship.
>
> (Birdwood 1965: 221–2)

Travellers therefore listed distances, weights and measures, time for travel, currency, fauna and flora (Herbert 1634: 182–3, Fryer 1698: 34–5, 37, 178–9, 205–16), often arranged in the form of a table for easy comprehension also, therefore *limiting* in narrative terms the scope and variety that was the subcontinent. By mixing up personal observations with the so-called objective inventory, these texts hybridized the memoir with the database.

Aesthetic resignification

In an entirely different domain, that of art and poetry, we see a similar hybridization, but one that is embedded in an imperial and imperious resignification of a national aesthetic. My first example of this incorporation-resignification that hybridizes aesthetics in order to generate a certain imperial politics is William Hodges. Hodges, hired by Warren Hastings to provide the visual evidence for British rule's success, was much influenced by Mughal miniature painting. Mughal iconography, writes Natasha Eaton, was a 'mediator' for Hodges, albeit to prove that happy rural subjects (as seen in the miniatures) existed only in *past* art (2013: 130). Hodges seeks to capture the glory of an Indian past, and his register, cast in the 'rhetoric of ruin' (Nayar 2008). Now, the ruin was central to England's imagining of itself and was a strong component of the poetry of the age (Janowitz 1990). Indeed, the ruin was a symbol of the antiquity of the community and/ or the nation, and one could be justifiably proud of it. It was, in a

INTRODUCTION

sense, a *national* aesthetic. What Hodges does is to appropriate this aesthetic discourse of ruin and transposes it into India for entirely different purposes and with entirely different effects.

Hodges's travel narrative is replete with accounts of Indian ruins:

> At a little distance from Rajemahel are the ruins of a zananah, which I went from curiosity to inspect, as they are, when inhabited, sacred places.
>
> (21)

> Nearly in the center of the city is a considerable Mahomedan mosque, with two minarets . . . this building was raised by that most intolerant and ambitious of human beings, the Emperor Aurungzebe, who destroyed a magnificent temple of the Hindoos on this spot, and built the present mosque, said to be of the same extent and height of the building destroyed.
>
> (61)

> This hall was, by order of the Emperor Jehanguire, the son of Acbar, highly decorated with painting and gilding; but in the lapse of time it was found to be gone greatly to decay; and the Emperor Aurungzebe, either from superstition or avarice, ordered it to be entirely defaced, and the walls whitened.
>
> (119–20)

> This fine country exhibits, in its present state, a melancholy proof of the consequences of a bad government, of wild ambition, and the horrors attending civil dissensions; for when the governors of this country were in plenitude of power, and exercised their rights with wisdom, from the excellence of its climate, with some degree of industry, it must have been a perfect garden; but now all is desolation and silence.
>
> (121)

The transnationalization of the aesthetic mode resignifies the ruin as evidence of India's despotic rulers, the collapse of civilization and decaying social order – all of which necessitate British rule and intervention. When the aesthetic is transplanted, therefore, its politics changes almost entirely. Whereas in Britain it energized a cultural pride in the legacy of ancient glories, in India it induced melancholy (in Hodges) and only bespoke the irretrievable collapse of Indian society.

INTRODUCTION

In other words, Hodges translates and transforms a national aesthetic into an imperial aesthetic.

My next illustration for the resignification of a national aesthetic as an imperial aesthetic is Felicia Hemans's narrative poem, 'The Indian City'. Felicia Hemans presented herself as a nationalist and a patriot (Lootens 1994). In 'The Indian City', Hemans offers a model of female heroism in Maimuna and attributes the collapse of the Oriental City to Maimuna's actions. Hemans achieves this by appropriating Britain's national aesthetic of the picturesque and resignifying it into an imperial one. The picturesque was used to represent English landscape (Andrews 1989, Copley and Garside 1994). Hemans offers a natural picturesque in descriptions like these:

> the plantain glitter'd with leaves of gold,
> As a tree midst the genii-gardens old,
> And the cypress lifted a blazing spire,
> And the stems of the cocoas were shafts of fire.
> Many a white pagoda's gleam.

And

> He gazed where the stately city rose
> Like a pageant of clouds in its red repose . . .
> He track'd the brink of the shining lake,
> By the tall canes feathr'd in tuft and brake.

After the young boy's death and the mother's rage, the aesthetic of the poem shifts into a ruin picturesque:

> Palace and tower on that plain were left,
> Like fallen trees by the lightning cleft;
> The wild vine mantled the stately square,
> The Rajah's throne was the serpent's lair,
> And the jungle grass o'er the altar sprung–
> This was the work of one deep heart wrung.

As I have proposed elsewhere (Nayar 2015), the picturesque landscape at the end of the poem has changed from the passive but *prosperous Hindu city* to a *Muslim ruin*, and Hemans thereby maps a moral geography of the land. The Hindu city had offered a sleepy but secure landscape, while the Muslims had destroyed the land entirely, except for the graves. Hemans appropriates a national aesthetic that was deployed in Britain through the eighteenth century and well into the nineteenth to speak of the countryside, gentlemanly sensibilities and generated icons for public approval and converts it into an imperial one here. In Hemans's imperial version of the national aesthetic, she achieves the colonial end: of demonstrating the ruins of the subcontinent that then lay the foundations for the colonial rhetoric of the civilizational mission.

The grammar and lexicon of Empire

Grammars were integral to the imperial archive and scriptorial foundations because the English needed to understand the native languages and devise its own in order to negotiate and administer. John Gilchrist published *A Grammar of the Hindoostanee Language* in 1796, adapting the work of George Hadley who had published his *Grammatical Remarks on the Practical and Vulgar Dialect of the Indostan Language, Commonly Called Moors* (1772). By 1801 written examinations to test proficiency in Hindustani among potential Company employees were already in place, and candidates at Haileybury were expected to translate from Hindustani into English and vice versa. Initial works on the Hindustani language were directed at acquiring enough linguistic proficiency so as to issue orders, as Peter Friedlander has noted (2006).

If grammars were focused on linguistic competence, cultural competence required a larger playing field. Specialized handbooks and dictionaries, such as George Watt's *A Dictionary of the Economic Products of India* (1885), appeared through the latter half of the nineteenth century. George Clifford Whitworth's *An Anglo-Indian Dictionary* (1885) anticipated the necessity of a Raj lexicon. Colloquial words and terms that provided a form of social grease in conversations with native (colonized) subjects demanded a reliable dictionary or glossary. Official jargon also necessitated a definitive guide. This meant that a dictionary or lexicon needed to serve not only as a linguistic compendium but also offer a text for cultural literacy. It is in this context that we need to see A.C. Burnell and Henry Yule's classic, *Hobson-Jobson* (1886). It may have taken its inspiration from Victorian lexicography but itself defied classification, as Kate Teltscher in her Introduction to the Oxford World Classics edition of *Hobson-Jobson* (2015) points out. Cast within the expected arrogance of imperial discourse (Teltscher: xx), *Hobson-Jobson* offers an amazing cultural history in its lexicon, anecdotes, brief histories and comments. The work is an entry point into the cultures of the Raj.

Such compendia and dictionaries were also cross-over genres. The colonial/imperial public sphere was constituted through textual exchanges, and very often these exchanges were *cross-cultural, generically polyphonic, transmedial* and *discursively multilayered*. Thus local oral and folk texts entered English print cultures, and those, in turn, made up a public sphere for debates, discussions and policy-making. While ostensibly about economic products or linguistic features, these glossaries and dictionaries, especially *Hobson-Jobson*, were portable *cultural histories* for imperialists. They sourced information from native texts and European ones. They indulged in speculations and cited earlier meanings. They claimed scientific reliability and cited official documents.

Dictionaries such as *Hobson-Jobson* documented the words and terms that the British used to describe and define the subcontinent in their aesthetic, administrative, literary texts, commentaries and dictionaries. These words were not simply linguistic and narrative acts. To return to Teltscher once again, the Yule-Burnell glossary was a 'record of the language of the Anglo-Indian tribe' (xxv) and participates in the ethnographic work around the colonial ruler and the colonized subject. This is precisely the purpose of an imperial lexicon: cultural work that sustains and reinforces administrative, economic and political rule. This calls us to address the dictionary of Anglo-Indian terms as not an exercise in mere historical linguistics and philology. We need, rather, to see it as an essential cultural exercise that was crucial for the continuity of power and a key feature of the imperial printextual public sphere, whether this was the power of early discoveries and settlement rights of the English 'factors' or the power of imperial commentaries on devadasis and thugs.

The imperial lexicon was deployed in ways that racially differentiated, administratively organized and politically subjugated the colonial subjects. Terminology and names carried the weight of imperial baggage and race relations, as the entries inside demonstrate. They did not always discern, they also discriminated (as Jacques Derrida once said about the language of Apartheid). Imperial lexicon and grammar were instrumental, in other words, in colonizing the subcontinent in particular ways: ordering, hierarchizing, instructing, commanding, dissuading, castigating, identifying even as it set about altering the native meanings of these same cultural practices. The imperial lexicon embodied, in Bernard Cohn's pithy formulation, 'the command of language and the language of command' (1997).

INTRODUCTION

It is important to note that this lexicon was not drawn from or meant to cater to specialized fields of study or enquiry alone: they informed *everyday* interactions of the colonial encounter. The British administrator was concerned that interactions with natives must be effective. This demanded, as John Malcolm wrote in his 'Notes of Instructions to Assistants and Officers', appended to his 1823 work, *A Memoir of Central India* (Vol. 2), a careful moderation in the British civil servant's behaviour:

> Our power in India rests on the general opinion of the Natives of our comparative superiority in good faith, wisdom, and strength, to their own rulers. This important impression will be improved by the consideration we shew to their habits, institutions, and religion, by the moderation, temper, and kindness with which we conduct ourselves . . .
>
> (433)

Such interactions required a functional *civil* and *civic* vocabulary, derived from both the Indian and European languages to generate a *lingua franca* of colonial India. In addition to the grammars and lexicon, there were also etiquette books and books of manners for both English and Indians, so that the increasing interracial interactions would fit into an acceptable set of norms of 'civil' behaviour (see Nayar, 'Civil Modernity', forthcoming).

Keywords in the imperial lexicon were those that entered into the cultural memory of the ruling race and became the sites of struggles over meaning: accepting native meanings, overturning native meanings, inscribing new meanings. That is, the imperial lexicon needs to be read as embodying and embodied in the social world of the colonial encounter. By resignifying objects or processes the British appropriated them in different ways for imperial purposes.

Questions of authority, prestige and rights determined the process of resignifying a native word for a commodity into an English term, or adapting a word from another source (such as 'compound'), generated an entire *cultural* logic of domination, a logic whose presence was embodied in the meanings and weight a word had to carry in the colonial era. The logics of trade, of government and of ethnography were all equally responsible for the pressure they brought to bear on the development of such an imperial lexicon. Properties of objects or their origins (say, for instance, *coir* or *coolie*) were accommodated within these logics and occasionally resignified. Often, for instance,

INTRODUCTION

the words had to account for Portuguese usage, European alterations and the Indian vernaculars. Where standardization was required, the various 'grammars' set out to do so (see the entry for *Hindostanee*, for example), formulating rules and norms as they went along. A single, irrefutable etymology was not always available, and so, in the identity and cultural politics of the colonizer, the words and their meanings were fused (not always synthesized) and took on hues of both etymology and popular usage: words like *batta* and *bahadur* in the Raj lexicon are instances of this merger and multi-hued cultural connotation.

Admittedly, the dictionaries, like the administrative tracts discussed in the early parts of this introduction, documented and evidenced the intertextual, often multicultural, provenance and nature of words and their meanings in the imperial lexicon. We therefore need to see the imperial lexicon as a co-produced – in terms of printing and publishing, European presses (missionary, government and private) also utilized Indian pressmen, compositors and binders (Starke 2009: 42) – and highly adaptive one since it made use of European and native vernaculars to forge new words and meanings.

This suggests that we see the imperial lexicon and the work of Yule and Burnell or Whitworth as not a descriptivist project but a prescriptivist one, for they determined *how* a word works and what its cultural significance might have to be and the social relations it needed to be conscious of, within the colonizer-colonized relationship.

*

The British Raj: Keywords undertakes a tour of the printextual public sphere of the British Empire in India, specifically its cultural lexicon. It utilizes imperial lexicography and in some cases philology to examine the larger cultural and political power in colonial word usage, naming and expressions. When, for instance, the town planners used 'civil lines', what did they mean, or understand, by 'lines'? What kind of public space did the 'gymkhana' signify for British and Indian patrons? Does 'maa-baap', as used by the colonial sahib, signify a specific kind of interracial relation? Does 'chummeries' call attention to a masculine ethos of the griffins in India?

Imperial lexicon as examined through the lens of postcolonial studies enables us to understand the political and economic ramifications of words and their usage. In order to further this end, *The British Raj: Keywords* utilizes critical commentaries on specific domains to illuminate not only the linguistic meaning of a word but its cultural and political nuances. This trajectory through the maze of Anglo-Indian

INTRODUCTION

colloquialisms and official jargon enables us to glean a sense of the Empire's linguistic and cultural tensions, negotiations and adaptations.

The British Raj: Keywords is a modest attempt at entering the cultural history of the British Empire in India through its lexicon and draws its inspiration from the genre of the dictionary embodied in *Hobson-Jobson*. Some entries have greater detail and information, others less so. This unevenness is because of a choice made regarding terms that have greater visibility and layers of signification when reading colonial texts.

This book is more a set of prefaces, or an index, to the texts of Anglo-India that one ought to read for this cultural history and as such is more indicative than illustrative. The extensive citations from primary literary-cultural texts are meant – to employ a culinary-gustatory metaphor given the dominance of the word 'curry' in colonial India's lexicon – to tickle the palate.

References

Andrews, Malcolm. *In Search of the Picturesque: Landscape Aesthetics and Tourism in Britain, 1760–1800*. Palo Alto, CA: Stanford University Press, 1989.

Bacon, Francis. 'Of Travel', 1625. Online. https://ebooks.adelaide.edu.au/b/bacon/francis/b12e/complete.html#essay18. Accessed 2 October 2015.

Bayly, C. A. *Empire and Information: Information Gathering and Social Communication in India, 1780–1870*. Cambridge: Cambridge University Press, 1996.

Birdwood, George (ed). *The Register of Letters of the Governor and Company of Merchants of London Trading into the East Indies, 1600–1619*. London: Bernard Quatrich, 1965.

Bolts, William. *Considerations on Indian Affairs*. London: Printed for J. Almond in Picadilly, P. Elmsley in the Strand and Richardson and Urquhart, 1772.

Buchanan, Claudius. *Colonial Ecclesiastical Establishment*. London: Cadell and Davies, 1813.

Carey, Daniel. 'Locke, Travel Literature, and the Natural History of Man', *The Seventeenth Century* 11.2 (1996): 259–80.

Cohn, Bernard S. *Colonialism and Its Forms of Knowledge: The British in India*. Delhi: Oxford University Press, 1997.

Copley, Stephen and Peter Garside (eds). *The Politics of the Picturesque*. Cambridge: Cambridge University Press, 1994.

Eaton, Natasha. *Mimesis across Empires: Artworks and Networks in India, 1765–1860*. Durham and London: Duke University Press, 2013.

Edney, Matthew H. *Mapping an Empire: The Geographical Construction of British India, 1765–1843*. Chicago and London: University of Chicago Press, 1997.

Fryer, John. *A New Account of East-India and Persia*. London: R. I. Chiswell, 1698.

Ghosh, Anindita. *Power in Print: Popular Publishing and the Politics of Language and Culture in a Colonial Society*. Oxford: Oxford University Press, 2006.

Halhed, Nathaniel B. *A Grammar of the Bengal Language*. Hoogly, 1788.

Herbert, Thomas. *A Relation of Some Years Travel*. London: William Stansby and Jacob Bloome, 1634.

Hodges, William. *Travels in India during the Years 1780, 1781, 1782 and 1783*. 1794. New Delhi: Munshiram Manoharlal, 1999.

Holwell, J. Z. 'A Genuine Narrative of the Deplorable Deaths of the English Gentlemen, and Others, Who Were Suffocated in the Black Hole, in Fort William, in Calcutta'. 1758. Reprinted in *India Tracts*. J. Z. Holwell. London: T. Becket, 1774. 3rd ed. 382–418.

Houghton, John. *A Collection of Letters for the Improvement of Husbandry & Trade*. London: Woodman and Lyon, 1728. Vol. 4.

Howes, Jennifer. 'Colin Mackenzie, the Madras School of Orientalism, and Investigations at Mahabalipuram'. *The Madras School of Orientalism: Producing Knowledge in Colonial South India*. Ed. Thomas R. Trautmann. New Delhi: Oxford University Press, 2009. 74–109.

Janowitz, Anne. *England's Ruins: Poetic Purpose and the National Landscape*. Oxford: Basil Blackwell, 1990.

Leask, Nigel. 'Francis Wilford and the Colonial Construction of Hindu Geography, 1799–1822'. *Romantic Geographies: Discourses of Travel 1775–1844*. Ed. Amanda Gilroy. Manchester: Manchester University Press, 2000. 204–22.

Lootens, Tricia. 'Hemans and Home: Victorianism, Feminine "Internal Enemies", and the Domestication of National Identity', *PMLA* 109.2 (1994): 238–53.

Mun, Thomas. *A Discourse of Trade to the East-Indies*. London: Printed by Nicholas Oakes John Pyper, 1621.

Nayar, Pramod K. 'The Rhetoric of Ruin: William Hodges' India', *1650–1850: Ideas, Aesthetics, and Inquiries in the Early Modern Era* 15 (2008): 75–106.

———. *Colonial Voices: The Discourses of Empire*. Malden, MA: Wiley-Blackwell, 2012.

———. 'The Imperial Picturesque in Felicia Hemans' "The Indian City", *Journal of Literary Studies* 31.1 (2015): 34–50.

———. 'Civil Modernity: The Management of Manners and Polite Imperial Relations in India, 1880–1930', *South Asia* (forthcoming).

Ogborn, Miles. *Indian Ink: Script and Print in the Making of the English East India Company*. Chicago: Chicago University Press, 2007.

Orme, Robert. *Historical Fragments of the Mogul Empire*. 1782. Ed. J. P. Guha. New Delhi: Associated, 1974.

Rennell, James. *Memoir of a Map of Hindoostan; or, the Mogul Empire*. 1788. Enlarged Ed., printed for the author. London: W. Bulmer for the author, 1792.

Richards, Thomas. *The Imperial Archive: Knowledge and the Fantasy of Empire*. London: Verso, 1993.

Steadman-Jones, Richard. *Colonialism and Grammatical Representation: John Gilchrist and the Analysis of the 'Hindustani' Language in the Late Eighteenth and Early Nineteenth Centuries*. Oxford: Blackwell, 2007.

Teltscher, Kate. 'Introduction'. *Hobson-Jobson: The Definitive Glossary of British India*. Ed. Henry Yule and A. C. Burnell. Selected by Kate Teltscher. Oxford: Oxford University Press, 2015. xi–xxxix.

KEYWORDS

Anglo-Indian
The term was used to describe Englishmen and women who came out and stayed in India for years. In the twentieth century, the term came to mean Eurasians: children of liaisons and marriages between the English and Indians. This latter is also the sense in which it is used in the Constitution of India.

Anglo-Indians include both nabobs and sahibs, with many of the latter coming from families whose several generations had been in Company or government service in India. Many established homes, social and sexual relations with Indians.

The Eurasians were also pejoratively called chee-chees.

Since Independence, the term Anglo-Indians has been used. They find representation in the Indian Parliament, by nomination to the Lok Sabha.

Ayah
For Anglo-Indians, the ayah was the centrepiece of domesticity in the colony, but is not to be mixed up with the 'ammah', the native servant employed as a wet nurse for the British children in Anglo-Indian households. The 'ayah' was used to describe the lady's maid but more frequently was the children's nurse and governess. She was effectively in charge of the children as a surrogate mother. Visual representations such as Joshua Reynolds's *The Children of Edward Holden Cruttenden* (1759) and *George Clive, Family and Ayah* (1765–66), Johann Zoffany's *Sir Elijah and Lady Impey and Their Three Children* (1783–84) and *Colonel Blair with His Family and an Indian Ayah* (1786), showed them as part of English family life in the colonies. Ayahs, in British stories and memoirs about life in India, were deeply

attached to their British wards, and fiercely loyal to them and their families.

Charles Doyley (1813) claims that the ayahs are attached to the children because 'the attachment is a principal source of amusement'. He writes:

> A total deficiency of education, the absence of every kind of rational recreation, except the game of patcheess, which is highly interesting, and possesses all the intricacy of backgammon, without its noise, compels the Ayahs into that habit of endearment and attention, which renders them far better calculated for the care of children, than our juvenile race of nurses, whose time is commonly divided between the novel and the window seat!
>
> (unpaginated)

The ayah enjoyed a fairly stable relationship with the memsahib: a relationship that gave the ayah considerable power over the other servants in the household. The English children often found it very difficult to part from their ayahs, especially when the ayah had to go on leave or the children were themselves sent away to England. Through the nineteenth century the ayah becomes a symbol of native loyalty in numerous fictional texts. She is portrayed as the conduit of information from the outside world, through the servants, to the Anglo-Indian family in numerous memoirs and fictional texts. The ayah saves the English children during the tumultuous days of the 'Mutiny', for instance, in James Grant's *First Love Last Love* (1868), Flora Annie Steel's *On the Face of the Waters* (1896), J.F. Fanthome's *Mariam* (1896) and others. In Alice Perrin's *Old Ayah*, the unnamed native woman cannot bear to go away from her wards even when her own (biological) son is very ill.

Ayahs also accompanied the English families to England, being deemed indispensable on the long voyage back. But, as commentators have noted, they were superfluous attachments once the family arrived in England and often treated badly (Visram 1986). They were often left to fend for themselves and find the money to return to India. In 1897 a home for ayahs was founded in London where they could stay until the passage home. Numerous advertisements with reliable ayahs offering their services for voyages to India appear in English newspapers during the 1880–1920 period, mostly inserted by English families testifying to the character of the ayah (Bressey 2013).

English children picked up Indian languages through their close relationship with the ayahs, and this became the source of considerable anxiety for the British in India who saw their children as 'going native'. Flora Annie Steel and Grace Gardiner's best-selling *The Complete Indian Housekeeper and Cook* (1888) was sceptical of the ayah – seeing her as too adoring of the English children and enabling a cultural hybridization of the ruling class. In *The Englishwoman in India* (1864), the author 'A Lady Resident', cautions: 'as far as possible children should be prevented from acquiring native dialects' (106).

The ayah can therefore be read as a professional, mobile colonized subject who possessed limited but potent agency in the English household, and whose presence within the domestic, intimate family space altered interracial relationships, especially of the memsahibs.

Baba

The term was commonly used to describe children, with 'baba-log' (child-folk) as a variant.

Baboo

From the late eighteenth century, it was a term to refer to the clerks attached to the East India Company and the government. Marked by their ability to read and write English, they were indispensable to the running of the imperial offices in India. The *Oxford English Dictionary* (*OED*) defined the Baboo this way:

> an Indian man (especially a Bengali) who has had a (superficial) English education and is somewhat anglicized; an Indian clerk or minor official who is able to write English; (in later use more generally) an Indian office worker or bureaucrat ... Frequently depreciative and in later use often offensive.

Over time the term was affixed to the Western-educated Indian, with a clear pejorative connotation. This stemmed from the Baboo's indeterminate identity, as a cultural hybrid. Augustus Prinsep's *The Baboo* (1834) was one of the first novels to deal with this figure, represented in the novel by Brijmohun Bomijee. Bomijee anticipates many of the later Baboo characters of colonial discourse: apparently servile but secretly treacherous, loyal by day and conspiring to overthrow the white man by night. Through the nineteenth century the Baboo would be caricatured, reviled and rarely respected.

The Baboo would not ever be fully white, yet had already loosened his connections with his roots due to Westernization. He was seen by the British as an icon of the 'monstrous hybridism of West and East' as Rudyard Kipling would famously call him. This cultural hybrid was imitative, snivelling, constantly seeking to impress the social circles he moved in, and aspiring to more Englishness than the English. Hurree Chunder Mookherji in Kipling's *Kim* is perhaps the best-known caricature of a Baboo. The Baboo flaunts his English, and his everyday speech is full of pedantic quotations, bombastic and hyperbolic usages and forced idiomatic expressions (documented in an 1890 volume, *Baboo English*).

The Baboo mediated between the white echelons and the native subjects and was often influential in imperial offices, courts and trading houses. He was thus the colonized native whose education and employment positioned him between a colonized servant subject and a Westernized native with a limited agency and cultural capital. While civilizing the native was part of the great civilizational mission of Empire, the Baboo comes to represent a figure who, despite his learning and Westernized outlook, cannot be fully accepted into the category of 'civilized' ('white but not quite white', as the critic Homi Bhabha described it). The Empire was therefore ambivalent in its perception of its own creation. The caricaturing of the Baboo emanated, critics have proposed, from this very ambivalence (Anindyo Roy).

The cultured, English-speaking native was a threat to the imperial social order and bureaucracy because English education had equipped him with ideals of law and order, autonomy and, more dangerously, nationalism. Hence, we see the Baboo represented as at once a necessary cog in the machinery and a threat. His nationalism was a direct threat to the Empire. The Baboo was figuratively contained within trope of 'effeminism' (Sinha 1995, Krishnaswamy 1998), where, by representing the Baboo as emasculated, in contrast to the manly Englishman, the Empire sought to demonstrate that he was unfit to rule despite his obvious Westernization. A well-known literary example of this trope is Girish Chunder De in Kipling's 'The Head of the District', where, appointed to the post of District Commissioner, De is unable to quell the civil unrest in the area. De is described as 'a gentleman . . . who had . . . a university degree to boot . . . cultured, of the world' (Kipling: n.p.). Kipling also describes him as a 'beautiful man', indicating his 'softness' and at the speech he gives to his subordinates, De is mocked by the latter, an omen for his later days in the administration. At the end of the story, the district is calmed with the following statement: 'rest assured that the Government will send you a man'.

Bafta
A kind of calico cloth from the Baroch area, its early description is to be found in the Dutch traveller, Linschoten in his *Itinerario* (1598). It had been a valuable component of export from India from the Mughal period. Bafta cloth was used as currency to purchase slaves in Africa in the nineteenth century (Sundström 1974). In the eighteenth century, bafta, along with calico, became a marker of status and class in English homes. The complaint that once-expensive calicos and baftas that were associated with aristocratic and upper-class homes, thanks to increased imports, now adorned the house of the common folk as well. Edward Terry who came as chaplain with Thomas Roe's 1615 voyage is contemptuous of this *laissez faire* of fashion around calico in his *A Voyage to East India* (1655).

Bahadur
From the Mughal 'bahadur' meaning a 'brave warrior', the term was initially used by Indians to describe Europeans as an honorific signifying gallantry. The East India Company was called 'Company Bahadur' by the Indians.

From the 1830s it was a rank and title conferred upon native military officers by the British government in India, Bahadur, Sirdar Bahadur, under the order of the British Empire. There was an entire ranking system of 'Bahadurs': the Bahadur, Bahadur Jung, Bahadur-ul-mulk, and others. There was also the Rae/Rao Bahadur (where 'Rao' signified 'prince') for Hindu bureaucrats and non-military officers, Singh Bahadur for Sikhs and Khan Bahadur for Muslim equivalents.

'Bahadur' came to signify authority for both natives and English officers, but in the case of natives, especially, it came to be construed as recognition of their loyalty.

Conferring titles and orders, including the famous gun salutes, were part of a colonial mechanism to bring together British aristocrats and indigenous elites in order to unify British rulers and ruling princes (Cannadine 2002). Indians of rank often competed with each other to ensure that such orders were bestowed upon them (CIE, KCSI, GCSI). It was an attempt to create a 'transracial hierarchy' and an 'honorific equality' (Cannadine 90). This hierarchy was made available in a compendium, Roper Lethbridge's *A Genealogical and Biographical Dictionary of the Ruling Princes, Chiefs, Nobles, and Other Personages,*

Titled or Decorated of the Indian Empire (1893) for reference, India's own Debrett's *Peerage*.

Such titles did not simply create an honorific equality: they were manifestations of the imperial politics of recognition. The indigenous elites, by accepting the title, conceded the right and power to the British to bestow the title, just as the conferring of titles reinforced British imperial and cultural authority, with the consent of the indigenous elites. Whereas in earlier eras and as late as the early nineteenth century the Mughals and indigenous rulers bestowed favours and titles upon the British, the British now assumed this role for themselves.

It was also a mode of separating and organizing indigenous elites through the tables of precedence where each native ruler was ranked according to the history of his family and the importance of his state. The tables also indicated where he would be seated, and when he would be introduced to the Viceroy. Further, the order or distinction could be enhanced or decreased at the will of the government. Families and kingdoms who had been traditional rivals now had one more domain to compete in: titles, honours and gun salutes assigned by the British. In short, honours and orders were useful as instruments of organizing social order and obtaining loyalty and favours from indigenous elites.

Bania

The British encountered the Hindu trader in the Gujarat area in the form of the bania. John Ovington records his views about them from his 1689 voyage. Later commentators such as John Malcolm (1823) noted the various caste compositions among the trading community in specific parts of the subcontinent.

The bania was favoured by British policies especially in terms of the legal security granted to debts and property. The British, especially when rebellion seemed on the cards in the mid-1850s believed the mercantile classes, the banias, would support the imperial powers. Later with the Mutiny behind them, trading and banking linkages were established between European banks and the indigenous banias. Scholars have noted how the network stretched from European, Bombay and Sindhi trading houses and banks to village banias, who were both merchants and moneylenders (Cheesman 2013).

Banias have also been stereotyped in colonial discourses as a greedy, unscrupulous trader who is forever seeking to ingratiate himself with the British officers. Banias as wicked moneylenders were commonplace in colonial writings of the nineteenth century. Since the bania was a banker, cash-keeper and accountant (as C.A. Bayly, 1986, shows), his role in food-grain acquisition and distribution was central to rural economies. Often, colonial texts portrayed the bania as profiteering at the expense of the village and the government (Bayly).

The bania enabled the colonials to stereotype usury as a component of Indian trade and mercantile attitudes, with the servile-yet-smart, greedy, predatory and monopolizing bania being the Indian equivalent of the Jewish Shylock (Subramanian 2012, Cheesman 2013). However, the banias also contributed to the building of canals and invested in agriculture for the local economies. They also exerted considerable influence over the local zamindars, who needed frequent loans and financial infusions to support their lavish lifestyles.

In the twentieth century the usurious bania would also be a regular stereotype in Bollywood.

Batta

Possibly connected with the Hindi word *battha*, which means extra payment, batta was an extra allowance paid to officers, soldiers or public servants over and above their salaries, especially when in the field and beyond the Company's territories. *Hobson-Jobson* connects it with the Kannada *bhatta*, which means rice in the husk, indicating a maintenance allowance, and was a term taken up by the Portuguese in India in the sixteenth century.

Batta was proportionate with one's rank in the army.

After the Battle of Plassey the European soldiers of the Bengal Army received a 'double batta', one paid by the Company and one by the Nawab, Mir Jaffar. In 1766 when the funds for this batta began to come from the Company, Clive abolished this double payment system in order to reduce expenses. Clive decided that those troops who were located in and around Calcutta – and therefore, by definition, not in the 'field' – would receive no batta, while troops in the proximate hinterland would receive half batta. Those in the field, that is at a substantial distance from Calcutta, say, posted in Allahabad, would continue to receive full batta. This reduction affected the lower ranks seriously. Wheeler notes in his 1878 work, *Early Records of British India*, that soldiers of the three brigades (Allahabad, Bankipore and Monghyr) rebelled demanding the restoration of the pay and were part of a 'secret league', even raising funds for their cause (1996: 342). The funds were to enable those who resigned from the Bengal Army to buy commissions in the British Army. William Bentinck as part of austerity measures in 1828 was ordered by the Court of Directors to reduce the quantum of batta by half for those residing within 400 miles of Calcutta, leading to considerable protests from the Indian soldiers in the East India Company army. Bentinck himself objected, but he was overruled in the matter in the Court of Director's final decision of 1830. The Company and government saved, according to a biography of Bentinck (Boulger 1897: 56–9), £20,000 annually as a result of this measure.

The Bengal Native Infantry's 66th Regiment was actually disbanded because they refused to serve without batta (Mason 1987, Heathcote 1995).

Bazaar

This word is from the Persian *bazar*, meaning a permanent market. It makes its appearance in European languages from the sixteenth century in the Venetian Caesar Frederic's account of his tours (1563–83) through the subcontinent, and in English in the early seventeenth century in the travelogues. The English document strange sights in Indian bazaars. For instance Ralph Fitch, one of the first Englishmen in India (1583–4), is astounded that diamonds are sold in the bazaars of Belgaum and calls the town 'a great market of diamonds, rubies, sapphires, and many other soft stones' (in Locke 1997: 99–100). Thomas Roe, ambassador to the court of Jahangir, described India as a giant 'emporium'. The bazaar represents, in colonial texts, the colours, noise and crowds of India.

The bazaar was a site of exchange and distribution and, as studies show, was a crucial mechanism in the linkage of the village to the world. The colonial romantic idea of the 'isolated' Indian village was a myth because the *haat* and the bazaar, the pilgrimage and the mela had been sites and modes of interactions and exchanges for a very long time. With the progress of the colonial state's dominance and intrusion further hinterland, the rural market was brought into its ambit as well, and the state forged links to these nodal points of distribution. Even in the colonial period the bazaar banker, however, utilized an older system of financial arrangements and exchange (Yang 1999).

The Indian bazaar was a place of dissipated lives, corruption and cheap mercantilism for the colonial. Novels such as Flora Annie Steel's *Voices in the Night* (1900) often represented the bazaar as the space of moral degradation, prostitution and ruthless commerce. In Steel's novel it is also the site of disease (the plague). In Steel's Mutiny novel, *On the Face of the Waters* (1896), the bazaar is marked by the prostitute and infection. Alice Perrin would embody the decadence of the English in her character of Rafella in *The Woman in the Bazaar* (1926). Rafella leaves the protection of her English home and marriage and, as Perrin's moralist novel suggests, 'lapses' into prostitution, becoming a 'bazaar woman' and thus blots the imperial escutcheon. Kipling would caricature the information system of the bazaar as 'bazaar gossip'.

In the nineteenth and early twentieth centuries, the bazaar would become the focus of imperial sanitation discourse, with the crowd and filth seen as sources for disease transmission. The regulation of this crowded native space acquired top priority in the nineteenth century, especially in the wake of the Mutiny. The colonial state organized bazaars around cantonments and native towns: special market areas where prostitutes could be housed and medically examined periodically (the *lal* bazaar), with the main bazaar being the *sudder* bazaar, and regimental bazaars which housed wives of the soldiers, but in some cases, also prostitutes for regiments on the move (Levine 2003).

Begum
From the Turkish, 'begum' was the equivalent of 'baig' meaning a higher official. The begum was usually of the upper classes, or of the aristocracy.

Bhang
The Hindi word for a preparation from cannabis and sometimes opium, used in food and drink, it entered the European lexicon through a Portuguese doctor who practised in Goa, Garcia da Orto, who documented it in his *Colloquies on the Simples and Drugs of India* (1563) and a few decades later in the Dutchman Jan Huyghen van Linschoten's *Itinerario* (1596), which presents a detailed account of 'Bangue'. The *OED* traces its English citation to Robert Burton's *The Anatomy of Melancholy* (1621), where he speaks of 'another [herb] called Bange, like in effect to Opium'. East India Company man Thomas Bowrey wrote in his 1670 tract *A Geographical Account of Countries Round the Bay of Bengal 1669 to 1679*:

> Sometimes they mix it with their tobacco and smoke it, a very speedy way to be besotted; at other times they chew it . . . the most pleasant way of taking it is [to] Pound a handful of the seed and leaf together, which mixt with one pint of fresh water, and let it soak one quarter of an hour, then strained through a piece of calico, and drink off the liquor and in less

than half an hour its Operation will shew itself for the space of four or five hours.

(79)

Robert Knox, best known for his 19-year imprisonment in Ceylon (1659–78), wrote of the medicinal properties of bhang being used to combat a wide variety of fevers on the island to Robert Hooke, scientist and discoverer of the cell. John Fryer in his 1698 diary of travels to the East Indies referred to it as 'pleasant and intoxicating'. Fryer was also extremely critical of the fakirs and other 'holy men' of the subcontinent because he claimed they were all bhang addicts:

> A fakir is a holy man among the Moors . . . Of this order are the most Dissolute, licentious, and Prophane persons in the World, committing sodomy, will be drunk with bang and curse God and Mahomet.

(196)

Robert Orme in his *A History of the Military Transactions of the British Nation in Indostan* (1799) claimed that the troops of the Indian kings would be high on bhang during religious festivals such as Muharram: 'to the enthusiasm of superstition was added the more certain efficacy of inebriation; for most of the troops, as is customary during the agitations of this festival, had eaten plentifully of bang, a plant which either stupefies, or excites the most desperate excesses of rage' (194).

Bhang becomes a key motif in the nineteenth-century colonial discourse when commentators such as John Briggs in 'Account of the Origin, History, and Manners of the Race of Men Called Bunjaras' (1819) claimed that these nomadic tribes were inevitably intoxicated on bhang. William Sleeman in *Thugs, or Phansigars of India* (1839) associated it with the 'criminal tribes', the thugs. Philip Meadows Taylor in his *Confessions of a Thug* (1839) also ascribed bhang addiction to these hereditary strangler–robbers. William Crooke in collection *The Popular Religion and Folk-Lore of Northern India* (1894) noted that animals like buffaloes, sacrificed at the first anniversary of any human, are 'intoxicated with bhang, or Indian hemp, and spirits, and beaten to death with sticks, stones and weapons' (111).

By the late nineteenth century, there was widespread concern about the abuse of even herbal cannabis, and the British government appointed the Indian Hemp Drugs Commission to file a report on the issue. The report (1894–95), running into seven volumes, concluded that suppressing the use of herbal cannabis would be unjustifiable and might raise tensions since it was acceptable practice in religious rituals. The report cited evidence where experts claimed that Indian soldiers were more prone to the addiction and led to criminal insanity (Singh 2014: 41).

Bhisti/bhisty

The water-carrier, he traditionally carried water in his goat-skin bag, called the *mussuck*. The bhistis were Abbasids from the Arab region. The bhisti was also required to sprinkle water in the courtyard so as to lay the dust, and supply water to the labourers.

The bhisti was immortalized by Rudyard Kipling in his famous poem, 'Gunga Din' (1892). In the poem, the bhisti is represented as fearless, catering to the needs of the soldiers in the thick of battle. Abused and threatened with dire consequences for any alleged delays by the soldiers, Gunga Din is unfazed by the bullets and shrapnel flying about him. Kipling thus compares his courage to that of a white man:

> 'An' for all 'is dirty 'ide
> 'E was white, clear white, inside

The speaker is injured and Gunga Din drags him to safety and gives him water, in the midst of which he is himself shot. But even as he dies, he expresses his wish, as a loyal servant, that the sahib liked his drink. Kipling concludes his poem with: 'You're a better man than I am, Gunga Din'.

Like the ayah, the bhisti in this case becomes the epitome of native servility and loyalty.

Bibi/beebee

The term is derived from the Persian word for 'lady' and often used interchangeably with 'begum'. The original sense signified a particular class.

By the nineteenth century, bibi came to signify something else – the Indian wives or mistresses of Europeans. The 'burra bibi' was the European wife or companion of the Englishman in India, but 'bibi' was the Indian woman companion/mistress/concubine. By the mid-eighteenth century, nearly 90 per cent of the Englishmen in India had either formally married Indian women or had liaisons with them. Colonel James

Skinner (of Skinner's Horse) was supposedly the descendant of an Englishman and a Rajput princess (although the British government denied this). Sir David Ochterlony often went out on a tour of the city (New Delhi) accompanied by his dozen Indian wives/mistresses.

Colonial writings constructed two major models of the bibi. In one, she was the epitome of self-sacrificing, docile womanhood (Sen 2001). In works like Flora Annie Steel's *On the Face of the Waters* and Philip Meadows Taylor's *Seeta* (1872), the Indian woman adores the Englishman as her saviour and gives up her life at the end of the novel in order to save him. The 'bibi' was all that the European woman was not. Lilamani, the eponymous heroine of Maud Diver's novel (1911), worships her English husband as a 'sacred subject' and is constructed as the very opposite of Audrey, a representative of early twentieth-century England's 'New Woman': feminist, pro-suffragette and independent. In the second model, the bibi was the seducer of the Englishman. Proceeding from the dislike of and fascination with the courtesan and *nautch-girl*, this model of Indian femininity was deployed to speak of the need to maintain English racial and cultural purity.

By the 1830s, therefore, such interracial liaisons were treated as signs of emasculation of the imperial rulers but continued in more discreet ways (Ballhatchet 1980, Macmillan 1988, Hyam 1990). The bibi was now redesignated the 'housekeeper', or asked to reside at a distance. Flory is criticized and mocked in Orwell's *Burmese Days* for having a native woman as the mistress. Progeny from such liaisons – the Eurasians – began to be seen first as the bulwarks of Empire and later as liabilities.

The bibi was always suspect even when she exhibited, as Lilamani does in Diver's novel, undiluted loyalty to the English husband. Nevil's family is certain that it is Lilamani who encourages George's (Nevil's brother) infatuation. The theme of the easily seduced bibi plays itself out in almost all colonial fiction and fits in with the stereotype of the oversexed Oriental woman (as early as the 1770s, Mary Montague had portrayed the Turkish woman in this fashion in her *Turkish Embassy Letters*). This fantasy of a docile yet seductive, visible yet private Oriental woman was the staple of colonial discourse (Yegenoglu).

Bibighar
It is the section of the house earmarked for the women. It enters the English social imaginary after the events at Kanpur (Cawnpore) in June 1857. Nana Saheb, having supposedly promised safe passage to General Wheeler's contingent, ordered the latter's massacre at the

Satichaura Ghat. Women and children, about 120 of them according to some accounts, were taken prisoners. They were imprisoned in the Bibighar.

Meanwhile Henry Havelock and James Neill marched toward Kanpur to recapture the town and won several battles against the forces Nana Saheb sent to stop them. Neill's approach was marked by extensive massacres of villagers en route, and news of his actions might have triggered Nana Saheb's response that culminated in the events of Bibighar.

On 15 July 1857, orders were allegedly issued to execute the women and children inside Bibighar. They were hacked to death by Savur/Sarvar Khan, the courtesan Husaini Khanum's personal aide. Their bodies were thrown into the well. When the British arrived in Kanpur, they discovered first the handprints of women and children on the walls inside the Bibighar and later the bodies in the well. Articles of clothing, hair and occasionally the dismembered limbs of women and children were discovered in and around Bibighar. J.W. Sherer records the sight:

> The whole of the court and this room was literally soaked with blood and strewn with bonnets and those large hats now worn by ladies – and there were long tresses of hair glued with clotted blood to the ground – all the bodies were thrown into a dry well and on looking down – a map of naked arms, legs and gashed trunks was visible.
> (Wilson 2011: 212–13)

'All the way to the well', wrote Captain Gordon, one of the first to arrive at Bibighar, 'was marked by a regular track along which bodies had been dragged, and the thorny bushes had entangled in them scraps of clothing and long hairs' (cited in Hibbert 1978: 209). Trevelyan writes in graphic detail in his 1865 history, *Cawnpore*:

> The sepoys were bidden to fall on. Half-a-dozen among them advanced, and discharged their muskets through the windows at the ceiling of the apartments. Thereupon the five men entered . . . Shrieks and scuffling acquainted those without that the journeymen were earning their hire. Survur Khan soon emerged with his sword broken off at the hilt. He procured another from the Nana's house, and a few minutes after appeared again upon the same errand. The third blade was of better temper; or perhaps the thick of the work was already over.

He then cites an anonymous eyewitness:

> 'The bodies', says one who was present throughout, 'were dragged out, most of them by the hair of the head. Those who had clothes worth taking were stripped. Some of the women were alive. I cannot say how many: but three could speak. They prayed for the sake of God that an end might be put to their sufferings. I remarked one very stout woman, an half-caste, who was severely wounded in both arms, who entreated to be killed. She and two or three others were placed against the bank of the cut by which bullocks go down in drawing water. The dead were first thrown in. Yes: there was a great crowd looking on: they were standing along the walls of the compound. They were principally city people and villagers. Yes: there were also sepoys. Three boys were alive. They were fair children. The eldest, I think, must have been six or seven, and the youngest five years. They were running round the well (where else could they go to?) and there was none to save them. No; none said a word, or tried to save them.'
> (Trevelyan (1894: 255–6))

This well would become, as Patrick Brantlinger argued in his chapter titled 'The Well of Cawnpore' (in *Rule of Darkness*, 1988), the centrepiece of British representations of the Mutiny (203). Stories circulated amongst the English soldiers of children's shoes with severed feet still in them, and children nailed to the walls with bayonets (Hibbert 213). Some diary fragments kept by the women before their execution and hand prints on walls were discovered. The soldiers who came into Bibighar after the massacre supposedly wrote their own messages on these same walls (Ward 2004: 439). All such narratives were calculated to ensure maximum outrage among the soldiers and the English back home and thus justified the massacres of the Indians that followed.

'Bibighar' and 'remember Cawnpore' became the slogans for the British soldier seeking revenge for the massacre of innocent women and children. The fate of Englishwomen was much disputed, as stories of rape circulated (Sharpe 1993, Paxton 1999). Stories of General Wheeler's daughter, Margaret Wheeler, who may or may not have escaped the massacre, became part of English lore. (Margaret Wheeler defending herself against the sepoys was the subject of a famous engraving from 1860; another story was that she married her captor and lived in Kanpur for years afterwards.)

Repercussions for the entire town were severe. Major Renaud and Neill executed sepoys caught in Kanpur and adjoining areas, with Neill making them lick the floor of Bibighar clean. An entire memory project came up around Cawnpore (Tickell 2009) in particular and the Mutiny sites in general (Goswami 1996).

In 1858 Robert Christopher Tytler and his wife, Harriet (who kept a journal of the Mutiny), photographed the area of the Bibighar gardens, as did Dr John Murray. Samuel Borne did a spectacular albumen photograph of the memorial in 1860. The well and Bibighar as icons in visual culture persisted well into the late nineteenth and twentieth centuries. In 1874 the *Illustrated London News* published a sketch, 'The Well at Cawnpore as it was in 1860'.

The spot eventually hosted the Memorial Garden. The memorial of the 'Angel of Resurrection', as devised by Charlotte Canning, was executed by Carlo Marochetti, with screens by Henry Yule and C.B. Thornhill. Sara Jeanette Duncan's *The Story of Sonny Sahib* (1894) deals with Nana Saheb's treachery and mentions the memorial but does not offer any details of the Bibighar massacre. In Paul Scott's *Raj Quartet*, Daphne Manners is raped in the Bibighar Gardens and her Indian friend Hari Kumar arrested and tortured for this. Years later, when Ronald Merrick, the policeman who tortured Kumar is murdered, 'Bibighar' is inscribed on the walls of his house, recalling both the instance in the novel and the historical reference.

Black Town

The name given to the Indian section of the town in Calcutta, Bombay and Madras Presidencies, it was distinguished from White Town and the cantonment. The creation of segregated spaces was a typical colonial move that helped administer these spaces differently and to regulate the native spaces far more stringently by limiting movement, crowds and entry into the white quarters.

In the eighteenth century, administrators expressed concern that the natives resided too close to British homes. An English traveller in Calcutta in the 1770s, Jemima Kindersley, recommended a fort for the East India Company servants, arguing that since Calcutta had no separate Black Town the 'roads [were] rather unpleasant' (1777: 277) due to the large numbers of natives one encountered. A letter from the Court of Directors dated 11 June 1800 expressed fears that the thatched roofs of Indian houses posed a fire hazard and so they needed to be relocated some miles away from British homes thus 'preventing or remedying the mischiefs arising from the erecting of habitation in Calcutta, thatched with straw and constructed of mats and other combustible materials' (*Fort William-India House Correspondence* XIII 1959: 206–7). Maps of the cities were prepared and boundaries demarcated.

In Madras, the British in the 1640s and 1650s lived inside the fort, Fort St George, and the natives outside, marking the Black Town. Later, the British also moved into the native sectors. Subsequent town planning, using the grid model, effected a transformation of Black Town, eventually making it a commercial centre (Talboys Wheeler's three-volume *Madras in the Olden Time, 1861–2*, documents these changes). In colonial Bombay too, the fort was distinctly white and separated from Black Town. Black Town was described thus by Robert Burford in 1831 for a panorama exhibition in London: 'the streets are narrow, the houses and huts closely built, and the whole thickly populated' (4).

Toward the late nineteenth century, however, the more affluent of Indians were allowed, even encouraged, to call upon the whites in their part of the town, and many wealthy Indians, in Calcutta, for instance, bought property in the white sector (Chattopadhyay 2005).

Bombay duck

It is a type of fish, also called bummelo. John Fryer, a seventeenth-century traveller, mentions it is his 1698 account, *A New Account of East-India and Persia*.

Boxwallah

The term refers to the itinerant merchants/pedlars who carried their entire merchandise in a box and therefore came to be known as the boxwallahs. They even developed their own brand of English, called 'Boxwallah English', which was essentially the language of trade.

Boxwallahs sold knick-knacks but also cloth and cutlery. Part of the great entertainment for the memsahibs was bargaining with the boxwallahs. G.F. Atkinson satirizes the enormous energies the memsahib puts into the process of acquiring anything from the pedlars in his *Curry and Rice* (1859):

> Mrs. McGhee is triumphant over the petty boxwallahs, those itinerant purveyors of lucifer-matches, ginger, salmon, castor oil, shaving-soap, pickles, note paper, and bridles. She despatches her emissaries (the Doctor's orderlies, who are enlisted, *vi et armis*, in her service), and the recreant pedlars are haled into her presence, to their unmitigated disgust, to

the general ransacking of their boxes, an abstraction, at nominal prices, of their choicest treasures, with hopes faint and undefined of pecuniary compensation.
(unpaginated)

The boxwallah figures in Kipling texts such as 'From Sea to Sea', 'The Sending of Dana Da', among others.

Brandy-paani
It is a term to indicate brandy mixed with soda-water and was a preferred drink whether at home or at the club.

The brandy-paani (brandy-pawni, as it was spelt on some occasions) was an essential component of the Anglo-Indian, especially the male. G.F. Atkinson would claim that one of the signs of a griffin's having become acclimatized to India was when he 'has learnt to smoke, and polishes off his bottle of beer, or his brandy-and-water, in a style that would refreshen his good 'ol mother to behold'.

The junior English official's life in the colony was one of unrelenting boredom, and again, the brandy-paani was a regular feature of such a dreary life, as Lieut. Bacon's *Studies from Nature in Hindostan* described it:

> Their home is divided between a comfortless half furnished bungalow their stables and the mess house The day is spent somewhat as follows Parade at daylight idling perhaps a nap till eleven o clock breakfast at twelve idling till three after which tiffin and beer drinking and from four till sunset a game at rackets accompanied with cigars and brandy pani another parade perhaps or a ride until dark then returns the mess and wine bibbing until midnight
> (The Asiatic Journal and Monthly Register for
British India and Its Dependencies, 1837: 318)

Bucksheesh
Adapted perhaps from the Arabic, it meant a little cash present to drivers and helpers over and above their wage – essentially, a tip, as the Euro-American would call it. But it was also, as the European discovered, in many cases, a recognition of services rendered and thus a mark of respect or gratitude by the client, although in places like Egypt and India, traders, porters and beggars often asked for baksheesh as a form of gratuity, even when they had performed no service. Richard

Burton in his travelogue on Madina cites another definition: 'alms or tribute, which the poor Arab believes himself entitled to from every respectable-looking person' (8). In most cases, it was a payment for expediting services. This gave baksheesh the character of a bribe, and thus classifiable as corruption.

The British and Europeans in India often associated it with begging and money given as charity, although the practice was widespread in Egypt, the Middle East and much of the Eastern world.

Joseph Campbell titled his India travelogue, *Baksheesh and Brahman* (1956). He records being chased by priests for baksheesh and eventually identifies a 'baksheesh complex', which he saw as the characteristic of Indian 'poverty and squalor'. Campbell's definition of baksheesh was 'something for nothing'.

Budgerow

It is a longish boat, used to transport people and cargo in northern India through much of the eighteenth and nineteenth centuries. Occasionally they were also used as a means of relaxation for the British to sail down a water body at a slow, leisurely pace. William Hodges in his travelogue claimed that the British had introduced several improvements in the budgerow's structure especially in Bengal, in the form of a 'broad, flat floor, square sterns, and broad bows' (40). Hodges also considered these far safer than the others.

Budmash

In the colonial world, this term used to describe a variety of people, including gamblers, petty robbers, squabblers and con-men. It derives from the Arabic, where it signifies one who employs evil means to gain a livelihood. It was used as a generic term for 'ruffians' in the British Indian period.

Bundobast/bandobast

A word that enters the English lexicon from India, it meant anything from tying/binding to revenue and other forms of official settlement. It came to connote secure, efficient and disciplined, arrangements in colonial India. It now implies safety and security, especially in crowded and public conditions.

Bungalow

The word was used in India to signify houses built in the 'Bengali' style. *Hobson-Jobson* suggests that when the Europeans began to build their houses in India, they used the term to refer to this style. While *Hobson-Jobson* traces the usage of the term back to the 1750s, the *OED* pushes it further back, to the 1690s. William Hodges travelling through India in the 1770s speaks of 'buildings . . . generally raised on a base of bricks . . . and consist of only one story' (46).

For the British the bungalow with a compound was the basic residential unit in India. It was intended for a nuclear family, and the space inside was organized around functionality, as Anthony King (1984, 2007) notes. Thus the bungalow had separate 'rooms' for 'sitting', 'dining', 'sleeping' and 'bathing'. In these specialized rooms, the various functions are performed with equally specialised equipment such as 'cutlery', 'table ware', 'dining chairs and table' or 'sideboards'. The bungalow had high ceilings and large rooms. It was also, usually, bounded by a *verandah*, the space of certain kinds of social interactions and of the chotta hazri.

Later in the nineteenth century, the bungalow became more Europeanized, with Doric columns, pediments and balustrades in the regional models of Madras, Bangalore, Calcutta and Delhi. Variations of the bungalow in nineteenth-century India included the dawk/dak bungalow and the traveller's bungalow. In the east, with its heavy rainfall, the bungalow used thatched roofs, and flat roofs in the northern regions.

The bungalow was an architectural manifestation of the spatial separation of rulers and the ruled (British and Indians) and later of the various classes amongst Indians (Chattopadhyay 2005). After the Mutiny, the bungalows were grouped together into a specific area of the town to ensure easier policing and spatial control, and was designated 'Civil Lines'. While the civil bungalow recalled English rural residences, the military bungalow was a clear symbol of rigidly organized and maintained colonial space (Joseph 116–17).

It enabled the effective transfer of the ideals of British family space to India (Collingham 2001). The British in India transformed the bungalow into an architectural sign of its imperial power. The bungalows were used to house its officers and civil servants, but over time with greater concentration of wealth among the Indian elite, they began to acquire bungalows as well. The bungalow as the site of social occasions reinforced class distinctions among the British as well as racial distinctions between the British and the natives who had been invited into this space.

The bungalow came into literary prominence for a different set of reasons in the late nineteenth century: as the site of British deaths during the Mutiny and as a site of hauntings. Ghost fiction was set in abandoned derelict bungalows because, as one commentator notes, the bungalow was treated as the site of betrayal (by Indian sepoys) and of the deaths of innocent British women and children (Macmillan 1988). Bithia Maria Croker describes a traveller's bungalow:

> An avenue of feathery bamboos led to our destination, which proved to be the usual travellers' rest-house, with white walls, red roof, and roomy verandah; but when we came closer, we discovered that the drive was as grass-grown as a field; jungle grew up to the back of the house, heavy wooden shutters closed all the windows, and the door was locked. There was a forlorn, desolate, dismal appearance about the place; it looked as if it had not been visited for years . . .
> ('The Dak Bungalow at Dakor', *To Let*, 1906)

Later, Nellie and Julia in the bungalow see the ghost of a British man and his murder by a native servant. Croker, in particular, set several of her ghost stories, such as 'The Dak Bungalow at Dakor' in such bungalows, now seen as spaces reverting to their Indian origins and thereby slowly effacing the colonial master from its precincts. Indian nature eventually trumps the colonial presence, in such tales, and the ghosts are reminders of a past (colonial) glory. Kipling's 'My Own True Ghost Story' is also set in a dak bungalow. Its atmosphere is described thus:

> For bleak, unadulterated misery that dâk-bungalow was the worst of the many that I had ever set foot in. There was no fireplace, and the windows would not open; so a brazier of charcoal would have been useless. The rain and the wind splashed and gurgled and moaned round the house, and the toddy-palms rattled and roared. Half a dozen jackals went through the compound singing, and a hyena stood afar off and mocked them. A hyena would convince a Sadducee of the Resurrection of the Dead – the worst sort of Dead. Then came the ratub – a curious meal, half native and half English in composition – with the old khansamah babbling behind my chair about dead and gone English people, and the wind-blown candles playing shadow-bo-peep with the bed and the mosquito-curtains. It was just the sort of dinner and evening to make a man think of every single one of his past sins, and of all the others that he intended to commit if he lived.

The bungalow was adopted as a style of accommodation in England, where it was first employed to mark class status in seaside towns, according to Anthony King (1984), and the USA in the early twentieth century. Such a global adoption of this style of building, in King's reading, suggests a global culture built around consumerism and the accumulation of capital in the USA, England and Australia.

Burra bibi

Not so much a title as a term used to refer to the lady who claims precedence at any social gathering. Usually, this was in keeping with the order of precedence – the wife of the Commanding Officer at a station would automatically be the burra bibi – and social protocols of British social life in India, and the woman of the highest rank functioned as the burra bibi at any socials.

The burra bibi in any station would be invited to attend, inaugurate or preside over a variety of social programmes.

There might have been a slightly ironic, even pejorative, tone to the usage on occasion, when any memsahib sought to impress upon her fellow Englishwomen that she had a higher social standing. G.F. Atkinson in *Curry and Rice* (1859) satirizes the *burra bibi* in a station, depicting her as 'not entirely unconscious of the dignity of her state in life'. Atkinson writes:

> [her] greatest grievance being on the state of the Civil Service; and she bewails loudly at the cruelty of her husband not being a Commissioner, and avers that it was a most unjustifiable act of aggression that he was superseded, when he ought to be one of the Suddur, or, at any rate, the Resident of Horsepore, or Governor-General's Agent at Salaamabad; – and, between ourselves, I suspect she imagines he ought to be Governor-General himself.

Burra din

Any European festival or celebration, religious or otherwise, was referred to as the burra din by the natives in the area.

Burra khana

It is literally a grand feast, usually a celebration of weddings, birthdays, promotions and the like. These were elaborate affairs, and for many English officers and subordinates, a chance to ingratiate themselves with their superiors. But in many cases the protocols were too stiff, the food too rich (for India) and the heat stifling. G.F. Atkinson would mock the penchant for the *burra khana* as an exercise in excess – of pride, of snobbery and of gluttony. Atkinson's description of a *burra khana* at the home of the fictitious Byle family runs as follows:

> But the time would fail me to tell of how the feast progresses; indefatigable are the slaves in catering for their masters' wants, and eager in the pursuit of the choicest dishes, and vigorous in their contests for the cool champagne – which limpid beverage has had the charm of rousing the dull echoes; for now the conversation flows apace. Chumuch, the Griff, dissects the turkey, but consigns a pound and a half of stuffing into the velvet lap of the adjoining Mrs. Koofter; the flounce of the punkah becomes partly disengaged, and, after flapping about remorselessly like an unreefed sail in a gale of wiud, succeeds in whisking off the protecting wire-gauze top of the lamp, and launching it on the apex of Miss Goley's head, occasioning the blowing-out of the lamp, and the consequent oleaginous effluvium that proceeds from the expiring wick, to the general discomposure of the nasal organs. Then the punkah has to be stopped to undergo reparation; and frantic and awful is the heat that is engendered thereby.
>
> Then, after an interregnum of considerable duration, the second course is produced, succeeded by a pause 'more fearful than before'.
>
> The sweets have vanished, and at last the dessert, indicative of a concluding climax; the decanters are circulated, and the fair hostess telegraphs to the 'Burra Beebee' the signal for departure, and a move (in the right direction) is made. Then the gentlemen are doomed to a further session, which terminates in the production of coffee, when the gong tells its tale of midnight. The piano is heard in the adjoining room; some faint voice warbles a doleful strain, the 'Burra Beebee' rises, and a general dispersion ensues.
>
> Thus have we conspired with the good Mrs. Byle in the inauguration 'blow-out'; we have drunk her health in an early glass of cool champagne, and that of the baby Byle in a later bottle of a more tepid character: we have imbibed and feasted upon the good tilings that were piled upon her mahogany; but the heat of the room, we are thoroughly convinced, has deprived us of a stone of our natural weight. But we have

peculiar predilections, and do not recognize in her 'Burra Khanah' the most cheerful or the most delectable occupation to be experienced for the enlivenment of an evening at 'Our Station'.

In short, the burra khana was about an excess of consumption, with obviously accompanying quantities of wasted food, as some English commentators observed.

Butler English
Butler English developed as a dialect used for the interactions between servants and masters in colonial Madras. It is often classified as the Indian version of pidgin English. The 'butler' is the name of course derived from the head servant of the traditional English home. It is best characterized by the use of the *-ing* form of verbs. *Hobson-Jobson* notes that it also developed new jargon: 'family' for 'wife', for example (also Hosali 2000). Eventually 'butler English' began to serve as a code for 'bad English'.

Cantonment
The British demarcated spaces for its military personnel a few miles outside the towns and cities in India and called them cantonments. These were institutionalized forms of residence and settlement (King 2007). Several of these exist even today: Agra, Meerut, Bangalore, Lucknow, among others. These were walled-in residential townships and, over time, moved from tent-housing to proper buildings. These often had spaces for exercises, barracks, the mess, recreational rooms/spaces and were notable for well-kept roads and greenery (a feature seen even today in most cantonments). Officers had larger accommodation.

As early as 1765, Robert Clive in a letter to the Select Committee argued that one of the Company's 'earliest considerations' must be to 'station and canton the forces in such a manner as will best serve to defend the country and preserve the lives of the men' (cited in Jacob 1994: 93). The Court of Directors was also keen on such an arrangement for the 'service and good discipline of the troops' (Jacob 1994: 22). Consequently eighteen cantonments were set up by 1811, and the number grew to 88 by 1835 and 175 by 1860.

Some cantonments were intended to hold soldiers prepared for field operations, while smaller cantonments were designed to hold smaller numbers of soldiers for local work. Cantonments with exclusively European soldiers were intended for the former as it was believed right from the 1820s that only European soldiery can be entrusted with the task of keeping the peace in case of uprisings and unrest. In cantonments with a smaller number of Europeans the cultural practices of the sepoys were rarely interfered with. In others, European and Indian neighbourhoods in the cantonments were clearly segregated, a segregation justified in biomedical terms: Indian lines are pathogenic and English lines are hygienic (Peers 29–31).

The cantonment was also designed to keep the soldiers separate from the civilian parts of the town. Thus cities would be divided into two parts: 'city' and 'cantonment', representing the native and British imperial sections. Indians were not allowed to purchase or live in properties inside the cantonment. In 1839 Rooshum ud Dowlah, the former Prime Minister of Awadh, bought a bungalow within Cawnpore Cantonment but was denied permission to reside in it.

It was also a strategy to monitor the behaviour of the soldiers. For instance, the English soldier in India was notorious, especially in the nineteenth century, for drunkenness, gambling, visits to prostitutes and fights. There were, as a result, proposals to encourage activities such as gardening, theatres and reading, none of which really worked. The behaviour of the wives of English soldiers – some of whom took to prostitution – was also a matter of concern (Wald 2012). Regulation 20 of 1810 announced severe punishments for disorderly conduct within the cantonment.

Cashmere

From the name of the region, 'Kashmir', it came to be associated with the highly valued 'Cashmere' shawls in English and European texts from the seventeenth century.

Cashmere represents the circulation of colonial products in English markets and everyday lives. From cotton in the seventeenth century, through coffee and tea and now Cashmere shawls, the Empire's distant domains came, literally, home to the Englishman and woman.

For Englishwomen, Kashmir shawls added to their respectability (Daly 2002, Zutshi 2009). We can see this link between Englishness, respectability and imported colonial products – not to mention the aspirations of the English toward the acquisition of such products. In Jane Austen's *Mansfield Park* (1814), Lady Bertram wants her nephew, William, to go to the 'East Indies' so that 'I may have a shawl. I think I will have two shawls' (1970: 277). James Forbes spoke of the 'shawls of Cashmere and the silks of Iran' in his *Oriental Memoirs* (1834), indicating taste, class and wealth.

In Charlotte Brontë's *Villette* (1853), a working-class woman acquires a job in a Belgian family. Lucy Snowe tells the story:

> I think myself, she might possibly have been a hanger-on, nurse, fosterer, or washerwoman, in some Irish family: she spoke a smothered tongue, curiously overlaid with mincing cockney inflections. By some means or other she had acquired, and now held in possession, a wardrobe of rather suspicious splendour – gowns of stiff and costly silk, fitting her indifferently, and apparently made for other proportions than those they now adorned; caps with real lace borders, and – the chief item in the inventory, the spell by which she struck a certain awe through the household, quelling the otherwise scornfully disposed teachers and servants, and, so long as her broad shoulders wore the folds of that majestic drapery, even influencing Madame herself – a real Indian shawl – 'un véritable cachemire,' as Madame Beck said, with unmixed reverence and amaze. I feel quite sure that without this 'cachemire' she would not have kept her footing in the pensionnat for two days: by virtue of it, and it only, she maintained the same a month.
>
> (1984: 96)

Thus the colonial import is what lends a certain authenticity to English identity, whether upper-class men/women or the working classes.

Chappati

This leavened bread, described as the 'staple food of Upper India' in *Hobson-Jobson*, becomes central to the British imagination due to the 1857 Mutiny. Earlier travellers from the seventeenth century downwards had appreciated it as a wholesome item of food.

During the months preceding the Mutiny, chappatis circulated across villages in northern India. Villages received chappatis from an adjacent village, and sent out their own, in varying numbers. British officers intercepted the couriers carrying the chappatis, but could not quite understand the significance, although they did suspect that the message was encoded in the form of the bread. The Magistrate of Agra, Mark Thornhill, was puzzled to find four 'dirty little cakes of the coarsest flour, about the size and thickness of a biscuit' on his office table one morning, deposited there by his constable. The constable told him that a stranger had come to the village, handed over these to a man and asked him to make four such chappatis and send it to the next village (1884: 2). The chappatis were believed to travel over 100 miles in one night through this relay system.

The British could not crack the meaning of the chappatis, although many attributed it to some superstitious belief on the part of the Indians (the first sighting, by R.H. Keating, believed it was a native cure for cholera). At the trial of Bahadur Shah Zafar in 1858, the subject came up for discussion. At the trial, Hakim Ahsan Ullah, Zafar's physician said 'I consider that the distribution of the chappatis first began in Oudh'. John Kaye's massive history, *History of the Sepoy War in India* (3 volumes, 1864), also documented several eye-witness accounts of the circulation of the chappatis. Christopher Hibbert in his 1978 history referred to the 'great chappati movement'. Kaye's account is a famous one:

> From village to village, brought by one messenger and sent onward by another, passed a mysterious token in the shape of one of those flat cakes made from flour and water, and forming the common bread of the people, which, in their language, are called Chupatties. All that was known about it was, that a messenger appeared, gave the cake to the head man of one village, and requested him to despatch it onward to the next; and that, in this way, it travelled no one refusing, no one doubting, in blind obedience to a necessity felt rather than understood . . . The greater number looked upon it as a signal of warning and preparation, designed to tell the people that something great and portentous was about to happen, and to prompt them to be ready for the crisis . . . One great authority wrote to the Governor-General that he had been told that the chupatty was the symbol of men's food, and that its circulation was intended to alarm and to influence men's minds by indicating to them that their means of subsistence would be taken from them, and to tell them, therefore, to hold together.

After recording various current interpretations of the phenomenon, Kaye concludes:

> But whatsoever the real history of the movement, it had doubtless the effect of producing and keeping alive much popular excitement in the districts through which the cakes were transmitted; and it may be said that its action was too widely

diffused, and that it lasted for too long a time, to admit of a very ready adoption of the theory that it was of an accidental character, the growth only of domestic, or even of municipal, anxieties.

(Kaye and Malleson 1888, I: 419–420)

Harriet Tytler believed that, even though these were circulating from village to village, 'the officials took no notice of it . . . till after it was too late, when it was discovered to mean "be prepared for a revolution"' (*An Englishwoman in India*, 1986).

If chappatis formed part of an intriguing and intricate – but hiding in the open, so to speak, with the innocuous food item as a secret message itself – there were two other such objects perhaps performing the same function. One was lotus flowers, which also circulated through parts of India. The other was bone dust. It was believed that the British mixed bone dust (from cows and pigs to offend both Hindus and Muslims) in the flour sold in the markets.

For later-day commentators, the chappati represents the power of rumour in the making of the rebellion. Nationalist Hindu historians such as V.D. Savarkar (1909) interpreted the phenomenon as a sign of great revolutionary, and religious feeling. The chappatis might have been forms of information dissemination, but they were also modes of bringing together a public, as effectively as any social media. The objects which acquired meaning in the lives of people also brought people together, in ways we do not yet understand. But for Ranajit Guha (1983) and later Homi Bhabha (2009 [1994]), the indeterminacy of meaning associated with the chappatis was central to the creation of panic, which then drove the rebellion. In Bhabha's words, 'an old and familiar symbol . . . develops an unfamiliar social significance as sign' and this renders it 'awesome, terrifying' (2009: 289). More recent commentators have claimed the geographic circulation was not systematic (Wagner 2010: 65–6).

Chee-chee

Children and descendants of European-Indian liaisons, they were called Eurasians and later Anglo-Indians. Chee-chee was a pejorative term employed because it was believed, writes Ballhatchet, that 'they shared the vices of both races' (100). It makes its appearance towards the end of the eighteenth century.

The Eurasians were employed mainly in the railways but were also bankers, teachers, surveyors and engineers. They were known for a particularly striking accent, as novelist M.M. Kaye notes: they 'spoke with a lilting sing-song accent that was very like a Welsh one and was known as chi-chi' (1992: 194–5).

When the political and social tide turned against these racial hybrids and signs of racial 'contamination' (as they were perceived) the 'East Indians', as they called themselves, began petitioning the government for their rights. A petition presented to the Parliament in 1831 referred to their 'spirited and praiseworthy exertions to redress the grievances under which they labored, and to elevate themselves from the social scale, from the degradation to which they had been forced, by the ungenerous conduct of their European fathers' (Report of Proceedings Connected with the East Indians' Petition to Parliament, read at a Public Meeting held at the Town Hall, Calcutta, 28 March 1831, published in *Calcutta Review*, Vol. XI, 1849). The petition admits to a rather dissolute lifestyle embraced by the Eurasians: 'dancing and dancing and dancing, seems to constitute the sum of them'. They are heavily in debt due to their lifestyles and have ceased to be hard-working, admits the petition (85). The petition provides much of the stereotypes of the Eurasian community in India, even as it pleads for harsher measures to bring them back to disciplined work and productive use of their employment. Another report published by A. Nundy in *The Imperial and Asiatic Quarterly Review and Oriental and Colonial Record* (1900: IX, 17–18) noted that the Eurasians claimed to be 'of the same flesh and blood as the ruling race' (56). The report puts the figure of Eurasians at 120,000, of which many are so light-skinned that they 'pass themselves off as Europeans' (59). They 'bear European names . . . and adopt a kind of European dress, and speak a corrupt form of a European language, but in their habits and way of living they are strongly Oriental' (60).

This corrupted identity, as both the above reports propose, consigns the Eurasians to the lower strata of the social order in British India. They blurred the line between races, and between colonizer and colonized (Stoler 1989, Caplan 2001). Maud Diver's *Candles in the Wind* (1909) and other novels (*Lilamani* 1910, *Awakening* 1911) explored interracial marriages and their problems. In post-1947 fiction, Rumer Godden's *The Lady and the Unicorn* (1937), John Masters's *Bhowani Junction* (1954) and other works offered sympathetic portraits of the community. As Patrick Taylor would put it in the novel:

> We couldn't go Home. We couldn't become English because we were half Indian. We couldn't become Indian, because we

were half English. We could only stay where we were and be what we were. The English would go any time now and leave us to the Wogs.

(Masters 1983: 27–8)

Cheroot
Perhaps derived from the Tamizh *churutu* (literally, tobacco that has been rolled), the cheroot is a cigar clipped at both ends. The British took to the cheroot in India and Burma.

Chhota hazri
'Hazri' meant presence and 'chhota' was 'small' in Hindi, and the term was used to describe the 'little breakfast' of the Englishman, soon after waking in the morning. It included tea and cheese, usually, and occasionally a fruit such as a banana. This would be followed by a ride or a round of billiards with friends.

Chit
The chit was an important component of British life in India. A chit was given to a servant as a certificate, which could be presented to a future employer.

The chit was also a note sent by an Englishman or woman to another. This was often to set up an appointment for a visit, an introduction (for new arrivals in India) or an invite. Visitors would present the chits before they turned up at an English home.

Etiquette books were published that offered clues about the right tone and appropriate forms of address to be used in chits (William Trego Webb, *English Etiquette for Indian Gentlemen*, 1895, D. Brodie, *A Little Book of Little Manners for Young Indians*, 1912, Syed Fakhruddin Aboobaker El Edroos, *Modern Indian Etiquette*, 1922).

The chit also functioned on occasion as a promissory note with traders, with the Englishman sending a chit to the trader through the servant. Thus it was an instrument of credit for the Englishman at the local stores.

Chop-chop
It is a common usage employed by the Englishman (along with 'juldi-juldi') to hasten the Indian servant classes.

Chummeries
The chummery was an extension of the kind of accommodation for young scholars in the university where men were to share rooms (hence

'chums' and 'chamber-fellow'). In the nineteenth century, chummeries became a regular feature of stations and towns, where newly arrived young Europeans could be put up on a shared accommodation basis. The chummery was a lower-priced set of rooms, distinct from the club or the hotel (King 2000: 92).

Advice books on living in chummeries were published, with Leonard Julius Shadwell's *Economy of the Chummery, Home, Mess and Club* (1904) being a particularly popular one.

Chuprassi

The word originated from 'chaprass', the brass badges worn by servants to denote them as government servants announcing the office to which they were attached. The badge would be worn on a belt, a sash or a cloth slung over the shoulder. Others in private employment would wear coloured *cummerbunds*, sashes or turbans in the colours of their employers as proof of their affiliation.

Circuit House

A classic instance of colonial architecture, the Circuit House had high ceilings, verandahs and tiled roof. They were places that circuit judges, who toured the country, stayed in when in a particular town or city. The Circuit House functioned as an office and court when the judge was in residence.

In some cases, such as Delhi, the Circuit House was renamed Government House (in 1911).

Civil Lines

The British organized their lives in two spatial arrangements in the Indian cities: the Civil Station and the cantonment, the military base. The Civil Station was also known as Civil Lines. Anthony King (2007) writes that the use of the word 'lines' specifically referred to the physical demarcations of ground to indicate the location of tented accommodation in a temporary camp. Later these lines of temporary accommodation were made permanent and the term stayed.

Civilian

The term was in use from somewhere in the mid-to-late eighteenth century to distinguish those English in India who were not in the military services. These would be the employees such as **writers, factors** and later the Civil Services.

Club

The club, like the gymkhana, was an integral part of English social life in India. The clubs had reading and dining rooms, recreational spaces like the billiards room, smoking rooms, and in some cases guest rooms for overnight stay. In India the three oldest clubs were established in the first half of the nineteenth century: the Bengal Club (1827), the Madras Club (1832) and Bombay's Byculla Club (1833). There were sporting clubs, winter sports clubs (in Simla), flying clubs, football clubs, cricket clubs, drama clubs and others.

Benjamin Cohen's work on the associational culture of British colonies in South Asia also notes the arrival of transnational organizations such as the Rotary Club, the Freemasons, the Young Men's Christian Association (YMCA) and the Young Women's Christian Association (YWCA) in India (4). The clubs had their own crests, codes of conduct, embossed playing cards, neckties and so on, all constituting the apparatus of cultural citizenship in the colony. They were also meant to recreate European lives and recreational spaces in the colony, giving the expatriate English a sense of home and belonging. It was an important social space that partook of both metropolitan and the indigenous public spheres because, over time, this was the space where the English and the upper class of Indians interacted socially (Sinha 2001). It was also a space, therefore, of the crafting of an order of imperial etiquette, codes of interracial social conduct and polite society of the colonizer and colonized (Nayar forthcoming).

Must clubs, of course, were out of bounds for Indians.

Coir

From the Malayalam and Tamizh *kayir/kayiru*, mean cord or rope. Made from coconut husk, the fibre was exported to Europe from well before the sixteenth century. Marco Polo and Arab writings mention coir. The Portuguese traded in the fibre from Kerala/Malabar. John Fryer mentions it in his *A New Account of East-India and Persia* (1698).

John Gilchrist wrote of its virtues:

> This kind of rope is particularly elastic and buoyant floating on the surface of the sea to any extent Therefore when owing to the strength of the current a boat misses a ship it is usual to veer out a quantity of coir having previously fastened an oar or a small cask &c to its end Thus the boat may be easily

enabled to haul up to the ship's stern Were a coir hawser kept on board every ship in the British marine how many lives would probably be saved.

(1825: 289)

George Watt in his *A Dictionary of the Economic Products of India* (1885) noted that coir from the Cochin region was placed in 'the first rank' (2014: 422).

In 1859, American of Irish Origin, James Darragh and a trader Henry Smail set up the Darragh Smail & Company, India's first coir factory, at Alleppey, Kerala.

Collector

The Collector of Revenues in the British administration eventually came to be the local magistrate, and the term was abbreviated to 'Collector', and more accurately, District Collector.

The post of a district collector of revenues was the creation of Warren Hastings in the 1770s. Later they became the core of the Indian Civil Service, with revenue, administrative and judicial functions. Both the Diwani Adalats (for civil disputes) and the Fauzdari Adalats (for criminal disputes) were under the overall charge of the District Collector, although the latter was usually under the immediate control of an Indian officer assisted by maulvis and qazis.

Through the nineteenth century the Collector was more or less in charge of the government at the district level. He was paid, in the eighteenth century, Rs 1,500 as monthly salary and in addition got a 1 per cent commission of the revenues collected from his district. Cornwallis abolished the Fauzdari Adalats, replacing them with Circuit Courts with European judges. The Diwani Adalat was redesignated 'District Court' or 'City Court' and had a District Judge at the apex. This meant that under Cornwallis, the Collector had only administrative and not judicial functions. Bentinck reversed this and abolished Circuit Courts and entrusted their tasks to the District Collector.

The District Collector and Magistrate was a prominent character in Anglo-Indian fiction. Mr Heaslop in Forster's famous *A Passage to India* exemplifies one kind of British administrators with his clear rejection of British–Indian social relations and interracial cultural encounters: 'we don't come across them socially', he declares at one point. Heaslop elaborates: 'I've never known anything but disaster result when English people and Indians attempt to be intimate socially' (Forster: 161).

Indians were appointed to the position only toward the end of the nineteenth century. Through the nineteenth century the Collector was more or less in charge of the government at the district level.

Competition-wallah

The term was popularized by George Trevelyan's book of this title (1864). It referred to Englishmen who entered the Indian Civil Services through a public competition, first introduced in 1856. Before this competition, those aspiring for the Civil Services had to be nominated to the East India Company's Training College, located at Haileybury, London (one of whose principals was T.R. Malthus, who would go on to develop a theory of populations). All admissions and appointments were controlled by the Court of Directors. The patronage system was very effective here, and well-connected families almost always managed to have their progeny and relations nominated. There was a formal exam for the admissions, though. As Trevelyan puts it, this patronage system had its advantages and clear disadvantages:

> Now, the system of appointment by directors worked well, because it was founded on the principle of personal responsibility. Each member of the board wished his protege to do him credit. He chose the most promising of his sons or nephews: and a public-spirited man would often go farther and nominate the most likely young fellow of his acquaintance. The chief disadvantage lay in the fact that the lads, brought up in Anglo-Indian families, and among Indian associations, from an early age, looked upon India as their birth-right.
>
> (15)

The proposal to introduce an examination was forwarded by Thomas Macaulay and Benjamin Jowett, the Balliol College administrator and reformer.

Those who came out to India through this system of open competition, therefore, were not always connected to distinguished 'India families' (by which was meant British families who had served in India for long and often for several generations). The young collegians who came to India did not possess a ready social circle or familiar faces. As Trevelyan put it in his *The Competition Wallah*:

> The sensation of loneliness is much aggravated by the present system of selecting and training the members of the Indian

> Civil Service. In old days a Writer came out in company with a score of men who had passed the last two years of their English life in the same quadrangle as himself. He found as many more already comfortably settled, and prepared to welcome and assist their fellow collegian; and, in his turn, he looked forward to receiving and initiating a fresh batch at the end of another six months. Haileybury formed a tie which the vicissitudes of official life could never break. In the swamps of Dacca, in the deserts of Rajpootana . . . wherever two Haileybury men met they had at least one set of associations in common . . . Few of us are lucky enough to have more than two or three acquaintances among the men of our own years . . .
> (7–8)

The competition gave greater importance to the classics and thus enabled Oxford students to clear the examinations (Hagerman 2013, Vasunia 2013). Classical education enabled the making of solidarity with members of the ruling elites in India. It is even possible to 'wonder', writes C.A. Hagerman, 'if classical images of conquerors such as Alexander the Great, and of imperial peoples such as the Romans, had influenced Trevelyan's views of himself as imperial servant, and of Britain's empire in India' (4). The classics 'provided or ought to provide both standards of taste and models of social, intellectual, cultural, and political action in the present' (21). Even when the patronage system was replaced by the competition model, this insistence on classical knowledge remained more or less unaltered.

Yet the natives themselves, according to Trevelyan's character Henry Broughton (who writes the letters that make up *The Competition Wallah*), had benefitted from the English education since 1835 when it was introduced.

> The natives of India have, with marvellous eagerness and unanimity, abandoned the dead or effete learning of the East for the living and vigorous literature of England . . . Interest and ambition, the instinct of imitation and the thirst for knowledge, urge on the students; and, by the aid of a delicate taste, and a strong power of assimilation, their progress is surpassing to one accustomed to the very slender proficiency in the classical tongues obtained by the youth of England after a boyhood devoted almost exclusively to Xenophon and Cicero.
> (424)

The insistence on a classical education (intentionally) placed Indians at a serious disadvantage because they did not learn these subjects. When the competition was being proposed, William Muir suggested that Indians may be allowed to appear with Arabic, Persian and Sanskrit rather than Latin and Greek. After a review of the marks allotted, Greek counted for 600 and Latin for 800 (previously it was 750 each), but Persian and Sanskrit was worth only 500 each. English subjects (Composition; English Literature; Language, Literature and History of France, Greece, Italy, Rome, Germany) counted for 900 marks. When the age of qualification was lowered to 19, it automatically ruled out the Indians from the competition.

The competition's obviously exclusionary system was much criticized by Indians and some English. The Indian Civil Service itself was famously dubbed by Jawaharlal Nehru as 'neither Indian, nor civil, nor a service'.

Compound

It is a word of disputed origins but mostly attributed to the Malay *kampong*, although the traveller Bishop Reginald Heber believes it came from a Portuguese word for 'camp'. The term was used to refer to an enclosed space around a European house or factory in the colonies. In the urban setting the British lived in what Anthony King terms the 'bungalow-compound complex' (2007), that is a house set in enclosed grounds. King too traces the term to the colonial territorial systems of South-East Asia, alongside the **bungalow** and the *verandah*.

Congee

It is an English version of the integral part of the convalescent's diet: rice-gruel ('kanji' in Tamizh).

Coolie/cooly

A labourer hired to carry or transport materials, the coolie is not a skilled craftsman. The coolie bears the materials on his back, usually. Among the labouring class, the British noted, the coolie was at the lowest rung, and on par with slaves. The English writings on the term often linked to the Koli and Kol tribes of western and eastern India, respectively.

The term began to be associated with cheap manual labour performed by Indians and Chinese taken to the USA, South America and the Caribbean islands as indentured workforce. The trade in slaves and coolies was finally banned in the 1870s in America. Indian coolies were part of the workforce in Africa, Fiji, Ceylon, Burma, Dutch East Indies and other regions from the 1820s and 1830s, and nearly 30 million Indians were hired as indentured labour between 1830s and 1937. Driven out of their traditional occupations by the new capitalist processes of production, such labour was a way of employment for many poor Indians in the nineteenth century. The Indian subcontinent also replaced Africa as the source of such labour. The coolie/indentured labour system was part of the colonial era's global sweep and exploitative processes (Northrup 1995). Commentators have treated indentured labour as the successor to modem slavery and marked the Asia's integration into the world system (Mahmud 2013).

Conditions of work in these areas were invariably terrible, and the Indians, called *girmityas* and 'bounded coolies' in Caribbean plantations, were severely exploited. When the first batch of such coolies was repatriated to India (1871), their complaints ensured the setting up of a Coolie Commission in 1872. Its report recommended, among other measures, the maintenance of record books for hired labour, the regular inspection of estates by a Coolie Agent and provisions for the education of Indian coolie children.

In colonial representations, such as Charles Kingsley's travelogue *At Last* (1890), the Indian coolie was presented as more orderly, disciplined and docile, in comparison with the more recalcitrant 'negro' slave. They are even presented as happy at their labour. 'Coolie', 'slave' and 'labourer' were therefore stereotypes and categories the colonial regime constructed depending on their historical and material conditions (Kelly 1992). The rebellious worker, the recalcitrant native worker and the docile immigrant girmitya suited the necessities of plantations across the world – from the colonial tea plantations in Assam (Ghosh 1999) to the Surinam. Thus, the colonial text erases the conditions of coolie labour in favour of an ordered, even picturesque, English/European plantation (Döring 2003). However, the occasional insubordination and even rebellion in some cases (Malaya, Sumatra and other places through the early decades of the twentieth century) caused outrage and a combination of punitive and retributive countermeasures by colonial landowners and government. Such acts, moreover, troubled the stereotype of the docile immigrant coolie.

The term signifies cheap, and usually exploitative, labour even in postcolonial contexts – such as coolies at railway stations in India. In 2003 literary critic Harish Trivedi termed Indian call-centre workers, 'cyber-coolies', gesturing at the historical antecedents of colonial exploitations of the subcontinent's people: 'working not on sugar plantations but on flickering screens, and lashed into submission through vigilant and punitive monitoring, each slip in accent or lapse in pretence meaning a cut in wages' (Trivedi: n.p.). Amitav Ghosh's *Ibis* trilogy deals with the life of such coolies in Mauritius where, the coolie 'Asiaticks', as Mr Burnhan calls them in *Sea of Poppies*, replace the African slaves. Dr Goonam's autobiography, *Coolie Doctor* (1991), describes the life of an Indian doctor in Natal, with the title indicative of the associations of all Indians, even skilled ones, with cheap manual labour. Girmitya lives and stories are now studied as part of the Indian diaspora (Mishra 2007).

Coss/koss
A unit of measuring distance, roughly 2.25 miles in English units, and dates back to ancient India. The British continued to use the unit, often adding 'stages' to it. For instance, J. Postans, Assistant Political Agent for Sindh, writing in the *Journal of the Asiatic Society of Bengal* about the distance between Multan and Delhi, put it this way: 'Estimated distances 215 koss; 23 stages for camels; occupies from 23 to 26 days' (1841: 25).

Cot
From the Hindi *khatwa* and *khat*, the British often used it interchangeably with 'bed'. Thus we have Thomas Herbert writing in 1634 stating: 'the better sort [of Indians] sleep upon cots, or beds two foot high'.

Cotwal/kotwal
Originally the commander of a fort (*kot*) was a kotwal in medieval India. Later it was used to describe a native police officer. A version of the term also comes from the Turkish. The European use of it in India dates from the early seventeenth century and was used as synonymous with 'sheriff'.

Country
In British India this refereed to any local, that is, Indian product, as opposed to those manufactured in or acquired from Europe.

Country captain
A chicken dish that may have originated in the eighteenth century, and through the East India Company (EIC) sailor, arrived in the USA somewhere in the nineteenth century. It was a dish originally prepared with almonds and numerous spices. The term 'country' in the dish's title possibly refers to the common term for British EIC trade ships,

the 'country river' steamers that operated through the Hooghly and between Bengal and Burma. Their captains were 'country captains', and this particular dish, made from chickens or ducks, was supposedly a popular item on the menu at the Captain's table.

Cummerbund

From the *kummar-patti* or *kammar-band* (waist-band) of Hindi derived from perhaps the Persian, the cummerbund had been a part of the Mughal and Rajput costumes. It became a fashion accessory among the British officers and later a part of the uniforms in the American and European armies as well.

Before it became an item of style and fashion, the cummerbund also served a very different purpose. In the nineteenth century, flannel cummerbunds were worn as a 'cholera belt', a variant of the practice of wearing flannel next to one's skin, especially around the middle, in tropical regions (Cohn). The Murray's handbook for travellers to India explicitly advised the English on this point:

> Real winter clothing will be necessary if it is intended to visit any hill-station. Flannel or woollen underclothing and sleeping garments, and a flannel 'Kamar-band' (a belt of flannel 8 in. to 12 in. wide worn round the waist), are strongly recommended for wear at all times.
> (*A Handbook for Travellers*, 1911: xix)

The cummerbund became the subject of a satiric poem by Edward Lear, 'The Cummerbund, An Indian Poem' (1874). The memsahib is swallowed by a cummerbund, and since they could not find a murderer or any remains, they blame it on the native washerman, the dhobie.

> She sate upon her Dobie,—
> She heard the Nimmak hum,—
> When all at once a cry arose,—
> 'The Cummerbund is come!'
> In vain she fled: – with open jaws
> The angry monster followed,
> And so, (before assistence came,)
> That Lady Fair was swallowed.
>
> They sought in vain for even a bone
> Respectfully to bury,—

They said, – 'Hers was a dreadful fate!'
(And Echo answered 'Very.')
They nailed her Dobie to the wall,
Where last her form was seen,
And underneath they wrote these words,
In yellow, blue, and green:—

Beware, ye Fair! Ye Fair, beware!
Nor sit out late at night,—
Lest horrid Cummerbunds should come,
And swallow you outright.

Curry

From the South Indian *kari* (meaning, sauce), a dish, of either meat or vegetables, prepared with spices (especially chillies), came to be called curry by the British. It served as a *generic* term for Indian dishes. It is believed the British first encountered it in Madras in the seventeenth century, and the local version of curry powder, or in the Tamizh language *kari podi*. They also may have picked up the term from the Portuguese name for India's spice-laden broth, the *carrie* or *caril*.

The British in India, although aware of the regional differences in cooking, describe all dishes as curry. Lizzie Collingham in her account of colonial food habits argues:

> What the British in India ate, for breakfast, lunch, and dinner, was curry and rice. 12 Anglo-Indian dining tables were not complete without bowls of curry that, eaten like a hot pickle or a spicy ragout, added bite to the rather bland flavors of boiled and roasted meats. No Indian, however, would have referred to his or her food as a curry. The idea of a curry is, in fact, a concept that the Europeans imposed on India's food culture. Indians referred to their different dishes by specific names and their servants would have served the British with dishes that they called, for example, rogan josh, dopiaza, or quarama. But the British lumped all these together under the heading of curry.
>
> (2006: 115)

G.F. Atkinson in *Curry and Rice* (1859) termed it the 'standing dish of the East' (unpaginated). Later, it became a 'dish in its own right, created for the British in India' (118).

Dacoit

From the Hindi, *dakoo, dakait*, meaning robber, in English it came to mean a gang of armed robbers.

W.H. Sleeman created the Thuggee and Dacoity Department in 1835, and the Department continued its operations till 1863 when the department was finally shut down. Dacoits and thugs were closely aligned in Sleeman's operations (and that of his successors), evidenced in the title of James Hutton's work, *A Popular Account of the Thugs and* Dacoits, *the Hereditary Garroters and Gang-Robbers of India* (1857).

Contemporary historians and anthropologists have proposed that the groups of armed robbers might have been jockeying for power in the princely states (Freitag 1985). The colonial system made a crucial shift by classified the robbers as hereditary killer–robbers (Tirthankar Roy 1998).

Dak/dawk

It is the post or mail, delivered by men either on foot or horseback, in India and countries in the Middle East. During the Mughal era, dak chauks were maintained for the men who delivered the post. At the chauk, the carrier would hand over the mail to a set of waiting men and horses for the next leg. The carriers were named dak bearers.

By the 1770s, says C.A. Bayly (1999), regular posts with palankin and bearers conveying people and packages were established between Calcutta, Patna and Benares, and were extended to Hyderabad and Lucknow by the 1780s. However, the need for an independent postal system controlled entirely by the British government was noted. This was deemed essential because, as Bayly notes, the British discovered that the existing dak system was being controlled not by the Company or the local government but had been entrusted to landowners and wealthy men who acted as Head Postmasters, who in turn had hired the actual runners and carriers. This meant, as the British discovered, the Company's dak was being carried along with that of the Company's enemies because the same runners were being used. For instance, the north–south dak was controlled by Mohammed Waris and his family in Cuttack – who provided the service for both the Company and its enemy, the Marathas.

The dak system, as the British realized by the 1790s, was a crucial component of their nascent Empire. From this realization emerged a series of works documenting the dak roads. A. Upjohn prepared one of the first maps, *A Map of the Post Roads through Bengal, Bahaar,*

Orixxa, Oude, Allahabad, Agra and Delhi, in 1795. Through the 1840s and 1850s, maps of India with roads, dawk stations, post and bangy roads were compiled by James Wyld (*India Shewing the Post Roads and Dawk Stations*, 1848 and new editions in 1850, 1858 and 1860), H.G. Collins, Charles Joseph and others. By 1810, effective and independent dak arrangements were made between various stations and included Delhi, Mysore and Amritsar. The har-karas were also part of this information-gathering and information-disseminating network. The British streamlined the postal system, founded firmly on Dalhousie's belief that the railways, the telegraph and a unified postal system would be the 'three great engines of social improvement' in India (Adas 1990: 225). The postal system was overhauled in 1850. Dak used horses, men and mail carts. The term used to describe it was 'the dak is running' or the 'dak is stopped' during the Mutiny, the former implying that all was well, and the latter signalling that the rebels had blocked the roads and prevented the movement of the mail.

Special rest houses called dak bungalows came up as well. Dak bearers were posted along a road, and this arrangement made a considerable difference during the Mutiny in terms of communications regarding military movement, medical help and rescue operations. In the aftermath of the Mutiny, as rebels fled the subcontinent to Egypt, the Middle East and other parts of the Central Asia, the dak continued to operate. Seema Alavi (2015) in her work on Muslim cosmopolitanism in the mid-late-nineteenth-century India notes how tailors and others in Rawalpindi served as dak collection and deposit centre for the mail coming from as far as Patna and bound for maulvis and traders in the Swat region (55–6).

Devadasi

The Anglo-Indian dictionary, *Hobson-Jobson*, defined the devadasi as the 'slave-girl of the Gods' from the Hindi word. They were prostitutes in the temples of South India, according to *Hobson-Jobson*, which cites Marco Polo and other early texts on the devadasi. The term 'devadasi' itself, Leslie Orr (2000) has argued, is not found in Indian sources prior to the twentieth century.

The devadasi system was a part of the subcontinent's tradition, and devadasis were highly respected in societies for their art, since they were accomplished dancers. Even after marriage to wealthy patrons they pursued their artistic skills. Whether the term was also a caste-signifier – only women of a particular set of castes danced in temples – and whether the devadasi was also a quasi-religious figure are both matters of intense debate even today. As a recent study puts it:

> [Devadasi] communities have always occupied an ambiguous status in South Indian society. On the one hand, devadasis possessed a degree of social agency in that they were not restricted by the norms of patrifocal kinship. They lived in quasi-matrilineal communities, had nonconjugal sexual relationships with upper-caste men, and were literate when most South Indian women were not. On the other hand, records from centers of political power such as the court at Tanjore in Tamil Nadu document the fact that courtesans were commodities regularly bought and sold through the intercession of the court . . .
> (Soneji 2012: 3)

They were the subject of social reform movements and the Madras Devadasis (Prevention of Dedication) Act of 1947 outlawed the practice.

Visual and verbal depictions of the devadasis in the colonial archive consist of famous ones such as Christopher Green's *Representation of the Dancing Girls on the Coast of Coromandel* and Allan Scott's *Sketches in India; Taken at Hyderabad and Secunderabad, in the Madras Presidency*. Accounts of commissioned **nautch** performances at the houses of wealthy native sand kings and attended by the East India Company and government officials survive from the seventeenth century.

British colonial discourse merged the devadasi, with her quasi-religious devotional dance performances associated with temples, with the nautch-girl who was driven by economic necessity and was also, in all probability, a prostitute as well. The devadasi began to be treated as a prostitute in medical and legal documents in colonial India. Castes and communities of the devadasi system were also codified as part of this process of documenting native sexuality, especially forms of sexuality that the colonials saw as unruly and disruptive (Levine 2003, Tambe 2009). Women such as devadasis thus came under scrutiny for representing a form of native sexuality that was dangerous, unruly and even emasculating because the woman/prostitute was an independent creature. The devadasi, as Amrit Srinivasan's work (1985) shows, was also at the centre of economic transactions. Both Srinivasan and Gayatri Spivak (1996) argue that the men who urged reforms under the aegis of the colonial government were seeking to 'break' (Spivak's term) the devadasi's economic power (Spivak 140). For Spivak the devadasi was part of the mechanics of class stratification of women (141), a point that later critics such as Ashwini Tambe also echo.

Legislation against devadasis, such as the provisions under the Indian Penal Code of 1860 and Devadasi Act of 1934, were modes to regulate the lives of those women that fell outside the bourgeois marriage-family norm (Tambe 10–11). It ensured a dichotomy between 'respectable' womanhood and prostitution, with the latter coming in for stringent regulation and surveillance. Such dance performances – and this was not restricted to particular dance forms either (Chakravorty 2004) – thus began to be classified as 'shameful'. The Contagious Diseases Act was initiated as a means of regulating such women and their sexuality. Surgeon generals and doctors of the government sought to intervene in the devadasi system as part of such a process of sanitation, health and hygiene and were opposed by temple priests and others for interfering in temple customs (Soneji 117). Slowly, as the social stigma of the devadasi as a 'prostitute' was reinforced, the stigma adhered to the children of the devadasis as well, and they were consequently denied school education and such services. The 1947 Devadasi Act declared the practice as a cover for prostitution:

> Whereas the practice still prevails in certain parts of the Province of Madras of dedication women as 'devadasis' to Hindu deities, idols, objects of worship, temples and other religious institutions; AND WHEREAS such practice, however ancient and pure in its origin, leads many of the women so dedicated to a life of prostitution.
> (*The Tamil Nadu Devadasis (Prevention of Dedication) Act, 1947*: n.p.)

The devadasi reform movement, as commentators have noted, was at the heart of the nationalist project in the nineteenth-century India (Nair 1996, Kannabiran and Kannabiran 2003). The Women's Indian Association (WIA), founded in 1917, the All India Women's Conference (AIWC), founded in 1926, and the National Council of Women in India (NCWI), founded in 1925, all championed anti-devadasi legislation (Tambe 104). For the nationalists, the devadasi was important to their project of presenting a modern India. Janaki Nair puts it this way: the 'new nationalist patriarchy's "modernising impulse" . . . saw the resolution of the "problem" of the *devadasis* within the framework of marriage' (166). Thus the Devadasi Act's concern over the 'prostitute' was also coded as a concern over the marriage-ability of such women, as the Act stated: 'any women so dedicated shall not thereby be deemed to have become incapable of entering into a valid marriage' (Nadu: n.p.).

Dhooly/dooli/dhoolie

It is from the Hindi *doli*, a sedan chair type of structure, strung between bamboo poles, often used in British India interchangeably with 'palankin'. The dholi was more a portable chair than a palanquin. Paintings from the early nineteenth century, some composed by Tanjore artists, depicting an Englishman being transported by palanquin exist in the India Office (see Archer 1972).

The British army often used this as a vehicle for transporting injured soldiers from the battlefield, as Kipling describes it in 'Gunga Din':

> 'E carried me away
> To where a dooli lay,

The dhooly bearers or stretcher bearers were also seen in action during the Boer War in South Africa. R.V. Russell in his 1916 work *The Tribes and Castes of the Central Provinces* notes that the kharia caste were dooli bearers:

> The Kharias say that their original occupation is to carry dhoolies or litters, and this, as well as the social rules character. J prohibiting them from carrying those of certain castes, is in favour of the derivation of the name from kharkhari, a litter.
> (3: 452)

But, said Russell in the same volume, dhoolie bearers from the *kol* community were infinitely better: 'Kol bearers will carry a dhoolie four miles an hour as against the best Gond pace of about three, and they shake the occupant less' (3: 519).

Dubash

A man who could speak two languages (*do-bhasha*) was a dubash, a servant or interpreter in mercantile offices. He served as a broker and facilitator in these offices, acting as an intermediary between the Englishman and the native.

Ananda Ranga Pillai, famous for his multi-volume diaries, was appointed dubash to Dupleix in 1748. This is a routine term for a European in Arab and Asian cultures.

Avadhanum Paupiah, a Telugu, was a powerful dubash with Fort St George during the Holland brothers' time in Madras. Paupiah was later arrested and tried for conspiracy (1792), and the subject of the trial was documented in a book by David Halliburton (a Company official against whom Paupiah was alleged to have conspired at the Hollands' behest), and this book was co-authored by the novelist Walter Scott.

The dubashes flourished in the Madras Presidency, and at one point there were 12 dubashes working for the East India Company in the seventeenth century. They usually determined the outcome of an Englishman's decision because they could interpret the natives' request or offer. Over a period of time, this led to the term 'dubash' being used to convey the sense of a powerful, if manipulative and exploitative, native intermediary.

The dubashes were also, at least in Madras, traders, and Ananda Ranga Pillai had his own trading ship.

Duftur/duftury
Duftur/duftury in Hindi meant 'the office'. The duftury, or office-keeper, was a servant who worked in the office, whose principal job was to repair pens, dusting and binding records. Duftur records were often named after the place or location of the office. Both Hindus and Muslims, we are told by Charles Doyley in his 1813 work *The European in India*, were employed as 'duftoree', but they were not to be asked to sweep the floors or work with leather (for binding) (unpaginated).

Record-keeping was the principal function of the traditional duftur. Here is a description of the history of the Poona Duftur by J. Macleod from 1819, printed in *Correspondence Exhibiting the Nature and Use of the Poona Duftur* (1856):

> The Hoozoor Duftur is the record of the transactions of Government, as registered by the Government officers. In it were, kept all accounts of the receipt and expenditure of the revenues of the State, whether the realizations from the province or from whatever' source; the expense of troops, establishments, Inams, and, every species of grant, gift, and money transaction, whatever; excepting only the private affairs of the prince, or such accounts as it suited not the interest of individuals in power to leave on record.
>
> (1)

The document goes on to complain how these records were not properly maintained by Bajee Rao Peshwa. The British reorganized and restructured these native states' dufturs.

> Since the foundation of the Duftur establishment; under the [Inam] Commission, the Duftur has been completely examined and arranged into separate districts, and mostly also into Purgunas, and its arrangement by years also is in considerable progress . . . The Dufturs of the Konkun for the last ten years have been sent to Bombay. Abstracts of the produce, deductions, and net revenue of the whole country during the last year of Bajee Rao have been framed by districts, Purgunas, and Mahala, and in more than half the country by separate villages . . . Besides the records immediately connected with revenue, from which much matter still remains to be extracted, the Duftur contains many material of curious general information. Thus, the series of accounts of the districts and villages afford a view of the comparative state of cultivation and improvement, and assessment of the country at different times. Those of the armies and establishments, and particularly the Rozkirds, show the progress of the Muratha conquests and dominion, and the most important acts and events of their Government and the Turjumas furnish complete statements of their general wealth and resources.
>
> (1–4)

The British, then, appropriated the revenue and other records from the native rulers' duftur, codified and reorganized it for a clearer sense of the region's profitability. The native duftur was a crucial component of the British administration, as the 'Memorandum on the Poona Duftur' by Mr Chaplin, Commissioner of the Deccan, and submitted to the Chief Secretary, Bombay Government, makes clear:

> The utility and value of the Duftur of the Peshwa, for reference on a great variety of subjects connected with the territory of the Bombay Government, render it necessary to consider on what footing it shall hereafter be maintained, on the abolition of the Commissioner's Office in the Deccan. These records are now well arranged; and little difficulty is experienced in finding whatever documents are lodged in them . . . and is of much importance that they should continue to be kept entire,

and that Native Dufturdar in the immediate charge of them should be a person of integrity, with an establishment under him of an efficient description.

(4)

Chaplin's insistence on the integrity of the native officer in charge of the duftur was prompted no doubt by the significance of the records themselves. In cases such as the Poona Duftur, the archive was massive – '3,500 bullock-loads', says a letter in the above document (8) – and contained documents about landownership and produce that the British needed to scrutinize 'in order to prevent those frauds which may be al present so easily committed against Government' writes, C. Norris, Chief Secretary to the Government on 4 September 1835 (9–10).

The dufturdar was the native office in the Collector and Sub-Collector's office in the Bombay Presidency.

East Indiaman
Ships sailing under the charter of the East India Company, whether Dutch, English or French, were generically described as 'East Indiamen'.

In 1612 the Company constructed its docks at Blackwall, from where the East Indiamen were built and fitted out for a few years. Later, by the late 1630s the Company began leasing ships from various ships' masters. Due to the increased profits and volume of trade through the seventeenth century, the Company needed to expand. The Brunswick Basin industrial area came up around 1789–90, with timber yards, rope works, bakeries, gunpowder mills and foundries. East Indiamen were the largest ships of their age.

The time taken for the voyage from England to the East Indies was very long (a round trip took two years), and the Company sought to cut costs by placing as much cargo on every East Indiaman as feasible – by 1800 an average East Indiaman carried anywhere up to 1,200 tons of cargo.

They were known for a short period of time in the mid-nineteenth century as 'tea-clippers'. This term was first deployed by Americans because the speed of the ships ensured that they 'clipped off' the miles from New York or American ports to their destinations in China. Later there were 'clipper races', and even fights, between these ships sailing between China and Euro-America.

Some Indiamen built in India were used for the Company's trading voyages with China in the nineteenth century, but they were not allowed to travel to Europe.

Horatio Charles Hardy compiled the names of ships hired by the Company during the 1760–1810 period in his *Register of Ships Employed in the Service of the East India Company* (1811).

Eurasian
'Eurasia' in geographical terms is the combined land of Europe and Asian continents. The term is also used to describe people of mixed race, from Europeans and Asians. In colonial India the term was used to describe children of liaisons between the English and Indians – in the post-independence era they would be reclassified as Anglo-Indians. The Eurasians were pejoratively called chee-chees.

Factor
The factor, from the Latin *facit* ('to make'), was a commercial agent who transacted business for merchants back in England. The factor would work from a factory or warehouse and buy and sell goods for a commission. This was the traditional mode of functioning of the factor in Europe (Thomas Mun, the famous commentator on the East India Company, was a factor in Italy). But the commission system was deemed to be unsuitable for places like the Indian subcontinent.

In the 'factory' of the East India Company, a **writer** after five years in that position would become a factor. He would find buyers for the commodities the East India Company ships brought from England/Europe but also suppliers for what the Company wanted to purchase – such as spices, fabrics, tea – and take back to Europe. Both commodities would be stored in the factory, until such time as the buyer and seller prices were negotiated by the factor.

The factors often undertook private trading for their own profits – despite being salaried employees of the Company, but also given some share in the stock – and thereby deprived the Company of the same. Suspicion was always centred on the integrity of the factors (Chaudhuri 1965: 74). Through the seventeenth century, the powers of the factors increased as the Company relied more on them than the Fleet Commanders of the ships to perform the trading functions.

K.N. Chaudhuri notes how the Company tried very hard to select factors of a good record and relatively honest dispositions, but were not always successful (80–1). With their salary and their rising stock, the factors often made decent profits, but most of them were always willing to indulge in some private trading as well.

The factors were known for revelry with local women and often attracted notoriety for their behaviour in public (Dalrymple 2004: 16).

The factors were also from the early decades of the seventeenth century, involved with Indian women, or bibis, in either concubinage or marriage. The first documented case of an official marriage between an English factor and an Indian woman is that of John Leachland in 1626. In Peter Mundy's *The Travels of Peter Mundy in Europe and Asia, 1608–1667*, he cites the Leachland case:

> John Letchland having for some passed years privately kept a Woman of this Country and by her had a Childe (lately deceased) whereby it was discovered to the rest of the English, with whom also he still continues. And notwithstanding the many persuasions both of the President and Council to divert him from farther persisting in that Course of life, stands yet see firmly resolute not to leave her, as that he desires rather to be Suspended the Company's service and wages then to be constrained to abandon her conversation, though with Continuance of his wonted means and former repute, which desire of his being by this Council had to consideration, it was concluded to condescend to his request until the Company's farther pleasure be manifested. The rather for that any strict course would (as his passions declare) have hastened his marrying to her and so consequently have forsaken his country and friends; or in case of fail thereof to some other desperate undertaking to his apparent ruin, both which all were willing to prevent, hoping that time will reclaim him and that himself will at last be sensible of his own errors, being otherwise a man of fair demeanour, sufficient abilities, and clear of accounts with the Honorable Company in India . . .
> (Mundy 1907, Vol 2: 354–5)

Such behaviour of the factors in the subcontinent was a matter of some concern to the Company. Drunken brawls and corruption were common charges levelled against them. Accounts of their behaviour appear in documents such as *Letters Received by the East India Company from Its Servants in the East*. 'By reason of drinking of rack excessively (whereof there is too much) most of our men came to their ends', says a letter about one such incident (190). An exasperated Nicholas Downton at Surat wrote on 28 February 1614 to Thomas Smythe, Governor of the East India Company:

> I wish you to have a religious care over the Indian Company's servants that are under your charge and let the evils of

others formerly make you more circumspect to have careful eye over the manners and behaviours both of young and oldest; and if any be found by excessive drinking or otherwise like to prove a scandal to our nation, I wish you to use first sharp reprehensions and if that do not prevail, then inflict punishments, and if that work not reformation, then by the first ship send him home with a writing showing the reasons thereof.

(31)

W.H. Carey in his history of the Company claims that alcohol and the hookah 'were consumed at all hours, from morning to night' (1906, 1: 99).

Factory
This originally meant 'trading post' and 'warehouse' in the seventeenth and eighteenth centuries. Ships arriving from England deposited their commodities here, and factors negotiated their sale. Surat saw the first such factory in 1620, and later permission was granted by the Mughal government to the East India Company to start such factories in Agra and Calcutta.

Fakir
One of the most popular figures in colonial discourse (Cohn 1996: 136), the fakir, literally a 'poor man' but often treated as a holy mendicant, was usually a Muslim (the jogi was the Hindu equivalent of the fakir). The sadhu, the swami, the jogi and the fakir were interchangeable in the English condemnation of *all* holy figures, most of whom appear mostly as bogeymen in the literature.

Christopher Farwell was appalled at the bodily mutilation of the fakirs and the native worship of such grotesques (1633: 27). Fryer says that their penances would 'make a man disbelieve his own eyes' (1698: 102–3). John Ovington observed that they 'gather a constant supply of dust and filth' (1696: 362). Ovington spent a great deal of time explaining the fakir's body (362–70), and claims that women and even wives are ready to 'prostitute themselves to the libidinous heat of wicked men' (192). Terry also described the bodily self-torture of the fakirs (1655: 281–4, 285–7, 293–4). Thomas Bowrey describes them as 'vultures' because they cause 'many injuries' to the 'poor inhabitants' of the country who are fooled into seeing them as holy (1997: 20–3). Fryer mourns that fakirs occupy the position of 'heroes or Demi-Gods in their superstitious calendar' (102–3). He terms them 'the most dissolute, licentious, profane persons in the world' (196). Edward Terry, chaplain on Thomas Roe's voyage to India, is appalled that the masses pay allegiance to such a man terming it 'wild devotion' (1655: 291). Similar accounts may be found in the writings of Alexander Hamilton, Francois Bernier and others.

For the English the fakirs represented an extraordinary spectacle. First and foremost, the discourse treats the fakir as a representative of India's superstitious traditions that allows the people to place their faith in such men. The fakirs symbolize the evils of native religions and belief systems founded on ignorance. Second, the fakirs represented a culture of indolence, sustained as the texts suggest, by faith, public endorsement and even royal patronage. India, in the guise of spirituality and the quest for religious icons, encouraged indolence, in the British view. None of these fakirs, notes John Fryer, among others, worked for a living. They represent, therefore, the prototype of the 'lazy native'. Third, and most visible in the nineteenth century, as characters in fiction, the fakirs became the embodiment of evil and horror (Parry 1998: 79–85). They are grotesque and frightening, especially to the Englishwomen. Alice Perrin describes an encounter of a fakir and an Englishwoman in 'Fakir's Island':

> Coming towards them was an ancient fakir, with one arm held high in the air, withered to a stick, and fixed in that position. As he approached, it became apparent that the nails had grown through the palm of the hand, and were protruding at the back. Following him like a dog came a small, humped cow; from its shoulder grew an extra leg, and from its forehead dangled another tail, both having been grafted into the little creature's flesh soon after its birth, – a very sacred animal, rendered still more holy by the cruel deformities that had been practised on it. The old man himself was a loathsome sight. His arm rigid, his long white hair caked with mud, his wrinkled body grey with ashes and hung with filthy rags. Chains clanked on his bony ankles, and he moaned dismally for alms as he proffered his copper begging-bowl to every passer-by. Behind him crawled a crowd of squalid, diseased, half-naked people – professional beggars. Some huge with elephantiasis; others literally dropping to pieces with leprosy, a few sightless from small-pox, and all covered with sores, and clamouring

for alms. The old fakir thrust his begging-bowl in front of Mona and gibbered.

(136–7)

Not only is the fakir described as a grotesque figure, he also becomes symbolic of something primitive, underscored by the use of the word 'gibbering', almost a pre-linguistic sound.

Fourth, their bodily asceticism – naked or partially clothed, unkempt hair, ash-smeared, etc. – appeared to the English as signs of depravity, moral decadence and the absence of culture (clothing being a marker of civilization and culture). Fifth, they were treated as criminals, extorting money from gullible people under false pretences or even murdering them. This interpretation, beginning from the last decades of the eighteenth century, resulted in the promulgation of laws in 1840 that categorized the fakir as a vagabond due to their itinerancy (Pinch 2006, Siebenga 2012).

The fakir was also a rebel or seditious figure in colonial discourse. The fakirs, who prevented from collecting alms and money from villages in the Bengal–Bihar areas, clashed with the police in the 1790s on several occasions. Subsumed under the name 'sanyasi rebellion', this was one of the earliest instances where the fakir is identified as a law-and-order problem in colonial texts. This image gains strength with the events of 1857 during which fakirs and mullahs were believed to have circulated through northern India instigating the natives to rebel. John Kaye's (1864) account of the Mutiny explicitly identified Hindu fakirs as causes of seditious behaviour. Ahmedullah Shah, called the 'troublesome fakir' or the 'maulvi of Faizabad', was also linked to the Mutiny especially in the light of his tract on Islam and his insistence on the need to throw out the British. Later, in the Afghanistan region, in 1897, a 'mad mullah' as he was called, revolted and armed a team of villagers to attack garrisons (Edwards 1989).

Fakirs as evil men with paranormal powers prone to curses and jinxes appear in innumerable Alice Perrin's stories: 'The Powers of Darkness', 'Caulfield's Crime', 'The Fakir's Island', 'The Spell', 'The Evil Eye' and novels such as *The Charm* all present fakirs with special powers. Perrin clearly situated the English missionary or believing Christian in some cases, against the fraudulent fakir in order to show a battle of faiths and civilizations. They are represented as vindictive and quick to anger. Thus, in 'Caulfield's Crime' the Englishman is punished for killing a fakir. In Kipling's 'The Mark of the Beast', the 'Silver Man' is somewhere between a leper and a fakir, and curses the Englishman for violating the sanctity of the temple. The fakir is described as a 'loathly' thing in 'The Bronckhorst Divorce-Case'. In his 'The Miracle of Purun Bhagat', unusually, the fakir, formerly Purun Dass, a native officer in the British government who had 'taken up the begging-bowl and ochre-coloured dress of the sunnyasi' (Underwood and Radcliffe: n.p.), is a hero.

Firangi/firanghee
This is a routine term for a European in Arab and Asian cultures, dating back to the ancient times. The term was used, often with some derisive content, for 'white skins' and as a marker of difference. Recent work in cultural history from William Dalrymple and Jonathan Gil Harris has re-evaluated the firangi.

As early as the fifteenth century, Vasco da Gama in his account of the voyage to Calicut (1498) reports that two of his sailors quit his services to join the rajah of Malabar. Perhaps the largest number of such firangis in the subcontinent was of the mercenary class, and who found employment in the Mughal, Maratha and other armies. Shah Jahan employed a large number of firangi soldiers and even had a firangi regiment. Shivaji employed several Europeans. The Dutch Eustachius De Lannoy commanded the Travancore army. Others were appointed to train the native ruler's soldiery. In the Anglo-Mysore wars of the mid-eighteenth century, the Mysore armies had at least 750 European soldiers. In the case of the Mughals and the Deccan Sultanates, many of the Europeans like Joshua Blackwell, Gonçalo Vaz Coutinho and Sancho Pires had converted to Islam, and thus fully integrated into the subcontinent. There are reports of at least five English soldiers who fought beside the Indian 'mutineers' and against the East India Company armies in 1857, one of whom, Abdullah Beg, has been identified as an Englishman, Gordon, who had converted to Islam.

Besides these European mercenaries, both Dalrymple and Harris pay attention to a class of firangis who spent practically their entire lives in India, assimilated into the subcontinent's cultural and other practices, including medicine in some cases, and died here. Dalrymple in *White Mughals* focuses on white officers like James Skinner who married Indian women and settled down. Harris in *The First Firangis* examines the lives of assorted Europeans who were mostly the typical ne'er-do-wells. Nicholas Manucci, for instance, was a Portuguese from a poverty-stricken family who arrived as a stow-away on a ship, settled in Madras and became renowned as a Siddha practitioner. Then there was Thomas Coryate, the 'English fakir' as he was known, who walked from England to India, was at the court of Jahangir and died in Surat. Thomas Roe records meeting him, and having dismissed him as a crank.

Thus for Dalrymple and Harris there was a class of firangis whose identity was not characterized by pure Europeanness or difference from the subcontinental races. Well before Richard Burton and T.E. Lawrence masqueraded as Arabs and 'passed' through hostile territory, there were firangis who adapted Indian and Asian lifestyles, learnt multiple subcontinental languages, acquired skills in native systems of medicine, worked with local rajahs and rulers in administrative and military capacities.

Fishing fleet

Marriage was a key social issue in the colony, more so than in England, according to W.H. Carey (1906):

> In no community . . . is there more married happiness than among the English in the East. Husbands and wives are more dependent on each other in this country than at home. There is no place in the world where a man stands more in need of the companionship of his wife . . .
>
> (1: 104–05)

The quest for suitable husbands among Company men was an intense one. The term 'fishing fleet' was used in a derisive sense to refer to single Englishwomen who were shipped out to India to find suitable husbands among the bachelor Englishmen. It originated, according to Charles Allen, sometime in the early nineteenth century (1977: 23). They were usually daughters of wealthy families living in India. Those who could not find husbands and returned to England still single were referred to as 'Returned Empties'.

Furlough

Traditionally the leave a soldier is entitled to. For the Company soldiers and administrators, this meant a trip to England and home, often at considerable expense. Some of the officers and soldiers were forced to proceed on furlough due to illnesses of various kinds, but also, occasionally due to misbehaviour (drunkenness, brawls, etc.). Furlough was also therefore treated as akin to a rest-cure, away from the stresses of the colony. A few Company officials, Waltraud Ernst notes, even feigned madness to obtain furloughs (110).

Garden house

In the age of the nabobs, particularly in the cities of Calcutta and Madras, during the latter decades of the eighteenth century the suburban villas were often described as garden houses.

Garden houses sought to mimic the gardens in England, with expansive grounds interrupted by flowing water with, of course, Indian species of shrubs and trees. The trees were very often mango and palm. The buildings were large, and the land area sometimes extended to fifty acres. Situated in the suburbs, the English travelled into the fort area from these houses. Eliza Fay in 1780 writes of the Calcutta garden houses:

> The banks of the river are, as one may say, absolutely studded with elegant mansions called here, as at Madras, gardenhouses. These houses are surrounded by groves and lawns, which descend to the water's edge, and present a constant succession of whatever can delight the eye or bespeak wealth and elegance in the owners.
>
> (131)

Lord Valentia notes that the houses are 'surrounded by gardens, so closely planted, that the neighbouring house is rarely visible' (Valentia 1811, I: 336–7).

Aristocratic and wealthy natives also built garden houses, and there are accounts of the Tagore house as a 'garden house', 'a beautiful and commodious structure, furnished in the best taste, and strictly in accordance with our ideas of Asiatic luxury', with 'gardens and pleasure-grounds being laid out in a style correspondent with the interior' (*The Asiatic Journal and Monthly Register for British India and Its Dependencies* 13 [1834]: 27). Swati Chattopadhyay has persuasively argued that the garden house of the native aristocrat represented an instance where colonial modernity enabled the landed gentry to separate themselves even further from the general masses of their own countrymen. Yet, argues Chattopadhyay, these garden houses were also spaces of contradiction where native values clashed with foreign ones and, ironically, the nationalist elite often gathered here to discuss their anti-colonial thought (2007: 170).

Gentoo/gentu

This term was used to describe the Hindu natives of the Indian subcontinent. It was, according to some authorities, a corruption of 'gentile'.

Hobson-Jobson claims it was a corruption of the Portuguese 'gentio' to indicate a non-Muslim heathen. The gentoos were deemed to be the aboriginals or original inhabitants of India. Indeed, commentators in the mid-eighteenth century, such as Luke Scrafton, believed that contemporary races and rulers like the Marathas had 'vastly deviated from the true Gentoo character' (1761: 15), thus implying a purity to gentoos as a race and culture.

Warren Hastings commissioned the translation of a Sanskrit legal text, the *Vivādārṇavasetu*, into English. A Persian translation was already extant, and the English translation came from the Persian source. The English document was the creation of Nathaniel Brassey Halhed, who titled it *A Code of Gentoo Laws, or, the Ordinations of the Pundits* (1776).

'Gentoo' as 'Hindu' was more or less established with Halhed's officially sanctioned translation. Halhed noted:

> With a View to the same political Advantages, and in Observance of so striking an Example, the following Compilation was set on foot; which might be considered as the only Work of the Kind, wherein the genuine Principles of the Gentoo Jurisprudence are made public, with the Sanction of their most respectable Pundits (or Lawyers) and which offers a complete Confutation of the Belief too common in Europe, that the Hindoos have no written Laws whatever, but such as relate to the ceremonious Peculiarities of their Superstition.
>
> (x)

Gentoo thus becomes Hindu (and Sanskrit) in Halhed's work when he uses the two terms interchangeably. Halhed stated unequivocally that codifying Hindu laws from its ancient Sanskrit texts was essential to aid British governance:

> From hence also Materials may be collected towards the legal Accomplishment of a new System of Government in Bengal, wherein the British Laws may, in some Degree, be softened and tempered by a moderate Attention to the peculiar and national Prejudices of the Hindoo; some of whose Institutes, however fanciful and injudicious, may perhaps be preferable to any which could be substituted in their room.
>
> (xi)

British governance, if founded on, or at least accommodating of, Hindu or 'gentoo' laws, Halhed believes, would make for a more peaceful rule, because the Hindu laws are intimately connected to their religious beliefs: 'they are interwoven with the Religion of the Country, and are therefore revered as of the highest Authority' (xi). Authorities like James Mill cited extensively from Halhed's work in his *A History of British India* (1818), although, as Tejaswini Niranjana points out, Mill uses this text (and Charles Wilkins's translation of the *Hitopadesa*) in order to demonstrate that Hindu morals and Hindu laws are both absurd (1995: 24). Indian legal experts, whether Hindu or Muslim, would be consulted for purposes of legal decision-making.

Above all else, the mystery of the 'gentoos' and their culture, it was believed, could be unlocked once the sacred gentoo texts were decoded (Cohn 1996: 21).

Later in the nineteenth century it acquired a degree of negative connotations. The native quarter of the town was called 'gentoo town', especially in Madras.

Godown

It is a warehouse, etymologically aligned with or derived from 'gudaam' (Hindi) and 'gudang' (Malay) and 'gidang' (Kannada).

Grass-widow

A pejorative term used to describe married women whose husbands lived elsewhere. It was mostly an appellation for those who went away to the hills during the summer while their husbands continued to live and work in the hot plains.

Its origins are uncertain and might have come from words signifying unmarried yet promiscuous women. H.J. Hervey in *The Europeans in India* (1913) describes the grass-widow with a measure of amused contempt thus: '[they] chiefly affect hill stations, whither they resort as soon as they are free of their husbands' (Hervey 1913: 125). Indian princes and rulers often tried to seduce such women.

Some of the grass-widows of the wealthier British led very comfortable lives, whether at the hill stations or when they went home to England. Alice Perrin's Mrs Warrender in 'The Pupil' recalls her days spent in London as a grass-widow: 'with a liberal allowance, beautiful costumes to display at Sandown, Hurlingham, Ranelagh – plenty of men friends on furlough to sit with her in the Park, drive her about in hansoms, take her in theatres, dinners, suppers'. Perrin's grass-widow fits Hervey's description perfectly. Such flirtatious, often middle-aged, grass-widows were the source of considerable anxiety. Indrani Sen notes how newspapers censured the activities of grass-widows for being unbecoming of the memsahib (18). Kipling satirized the grass-widow scene thus:

> The young men come, the young men go,
> Each pink and white and neat
> She's older than their mothers,
> but they grovel at her feet

His account of Mrs Hawksbee in 'Three – and an Extra' (*Plain Tales from the Hills*) became a stereotype of the frivolous, flirtatious grass-widow. Edward Buck in his book on Simla (1904) complained that authors like Kipling had ruined the reputation of the town with accounts of such grass-widows (168), even as he admits that the social life of Simla attracts more attention than its official one (169). Thus the grass-widow became the symbol of the frivolous Raj and an easy scapegoat for those aspects of the Empire that had gone wrong.

Griffin

The newly arrived Company official was called a griffin. They were usually unprepared for India and had to be tutored about protocol, rank, courtesies of the station, and cautioned against racial encounters, diseases and the manipulative native.

He would encounter beggars, mendicants, medicine-men and traders. He understood neither the nuances of bargaining in the marketplace nor idiomatic expressions. Very often he ended up with huge debts in his first year because he was persuaded to buy a horse, clothing, guns or carriage with a simple IOU (I Owe You) note (see 'chit'). Mike Dash quotes an English account of how the griffin was the object of ridicule and fun at the station because 'he fell off his horse, shot the wrong birds, he speared domestic pigs, he produced comic situations by using the wrong words and by misunderstanding Indian customs' (2011: 109).

A sustained account of the griffin's life is documented in Captain Bellew's *Memoirs of a Griffin, Or, a Cadet's First Year in India* (1880). It opens with a definition of griffin, by the narrator–griffin, Gernon:

> Griffin, or more familiarly a Griff, is an Anglo-Indian cant term applied to all new-comers, whose lot has been cast in the 'gorgeous East'. Whether the appellation has any connection

with the fabulous compound, the gryps or gryphon of armorial blazoning, is a point which I feel myself incompetent to decide. A griffin is the Johnny Newcome of the East, one whose European manners and ideas stand out in ludicrous relief contrasted with those, so essentially different in most respects, which appertain to the new country of his sojourn.

(1–2)

Bellew admits that these griffs were often very badly behaved: 'the wildnesses and consequent escapades of such boys have tended to lower the European character very considerably in the estimation of the Natives' (79–80). There is also the wide-eyed interest in India, the freshness of first impressions:

> Here and there, in front of a hut, mantled with its creeping gourd, would appear the milk-white cow or petted calf, picketed by the nose, and munching his *boosa* under the cool shade of the tamarind or plantain, whilst kids and goats, in various picturesque attitudes, sunned themselves on the ruined wall or prostrate tree. Sometimes we came on fishermen, in their dingies or canoes, with out-spread nets catching the much-prized *hilsa* or we looked on the dark peasantry in the green rice-fields, engaged beneath a fervid sun in their various rural occupations. Occasionally, we came suddenly upon a market, with its congregated fleet of boats, and its busy, squabbling assemblage of villagers, fish, grain, and vegetable venders, &c.; or a thannah, or police station, would break into view, known by its picturesque burkundazes lounging about in front, armed with spears or tulwars, and the portly, bearded thannahdar, *en déshabille* smoking his Julian under the projecting thatch of the entrance. The novelty of the scene, so truly un-English and Oriental, delighted me, and my heart bounded with joy from a feeling of vitality and freedom.

(184–5)

Later he describes mounting debts and accompanying melancholy. There are the visits to dancing girls, shooting and hunts, drinking and debaucheries which left the griffin with 'red eyes, trembling hand, and glued lips' (287).

Accounts of the griffins such as the above are useful to see how the Empire inculcated norms of race consciousness, hierarchy, social etiquette and imperial responsibility. The griffins were trained in the social schools – of clubs, 'At Homes' and social spaces where the seniors instructed them in the ways of the station. The griffin therefore represents the object of an imperial pedagogy and not simply a low-ranked functionary of the Empire.

Gymkhana

A sports club, often used to designate a gentleman's club and a privileged social space in the colonial era, the gymkhana club was established across India, Burma, Malaysia and other colonies from the 1840s. The term was derived from the Hindi *gend-khana* (ball house), gesturing at racket courts. Various sports, from polo to tennis, were played at the gymkhana.

Most of the gymkhanas were for British patrons only, although, ironically, these were often built through contributions from native philanthropists. The classic case would be that of Cowasji Jehangir, the Parsi philanthropist who donated Rs 1,000 toward the construction of the Bombay gymkhana club (1875) although he could never enter it in his lifetime. The inherent contradiction in almost all such colonial clubs – of racial exclusivism and multiracial patronage – is startling.

In many places, native religious communities, such as the Parsis, Hindus and Muslims, also opened gymkhana clubs, exclusive to the members of those communities. Such clubs were also participants and organizers of cricket tournaments and hosted local teams, like the Purushottam Shield Cricket Tournament of the Hindu Gymkhana, Bombay (Majumdar 2013: 143, n. 18)

Many of these clubs continue to exist in postcolonial India.

Hackery

They are mostly referred to the carts and personal transport, primarily bullock carts, or 'country carts'. John Ovington described hackeries as a 'kind of coach, with two wheels, are all drawn by oxen' (Ovington 1690: 255). Visual representations of the hackery were of two kinds. One depicted an elaborate hackery, complete with a roof, clearly intended for transporting people. The official draughtsman of the East India Company in Madras, John Glantz, in a series of lithographs, 'The Indian Microcosm' (1827), drew this model. The second depicted a vehicle for transporting goods and may be seen in Henry Beveridge's *A Comprehensive History of India* (1862).

Har-kara/hir-cara/hircarrah

It originally meant a courier or messenger, but also a spy and informant and maybe even translator for the Europeans. Their use by Europeans dates back to the eighteenth century when they passed on information about troop movements and reported on the developments in battle. On other occasions they were assistants to surveyors like Colin MacKenzie (famous for his Mysore survey), even going on to prepare maps of the territories (called har-kara maps).

The other sense of the term indicated the willingness and adaptability of the har-kara: they were people who could do everything and anything (can 'do all', from the Hindi). The information the har-karas gathered marked the first moments of the colonial/imperial archive with the natives converting themselves into native informants (Crook 1996). However, as Bayly notes, the har-kara tradition pre-dates the British, as Bayly notes, and there were stringent norms about qualifications for the job (1996: 64) because they were a part of the postal (dak) system. There were horse, camel and foot har-karas who constituted this network.

They were also used to spread information. Chris Bayly writes that the 'combination of har-kara information, newsletters and public recitations in bazaars' spread news across the country (200). The natives also restored the har-kara system during the years leading up to the 1857 Mutiny, according to historians (Rudransghu Mukherjee 2002: xvii).

Hawaldar

Under the Mughal and Maratha Empires, the hawaldar was the commander of a fort. When it entered the British Army it became a rank equivalent to that of a sergeant. The cadre still exists in the Indian Army but are more commonly 'junior commissioned officers'.

Hill station

In the early nineteenth century, the British in India decided that they needed to escape the heat of the plains during the subcontinent's furious summer. The original plan was to have sanatoria for the suffering English to recover, but eventually, the sanatoria grew into something larger. They founded towns on hills across the country and sent away their families to these 'hill stations'. Simla, the summer capital of the Empire, was the most famous of these. The hill station was marked by experiments in European-style architecture – Gothic villas, Tudor cottages, Swiss chalets, among others (Kennedy 1996).

The hill station was a closed community of the officers, their servants, their acquaintances. But they were also seats of recreation, relaxation and, consequently, scandals. The romances and extra-marital scandals of the hill station (studied by Indrani Sen 2002, for instance) were legendary. Kipling's *Plain Tales from the Hills* offers a glimpse of lives in the hill station, with its balls, at-homes, parties and birthday bashes at the club.

The hill station was also the site of imperial power, and the pantropical location reinforced the sense of 'overseeing' the subcontinent and its subjects for the British.

Hindustani/Hindostanee

The British could not always track the multiple origins of the language spoken in northern India, given that it had borrowed from Sanskrit, Arabic, Urdu and Persian. The term 'Hindustani' was used to describe this Hindi-Urdu. The British were also uncertain whether it was primarily a Muslim or Hindu population that used the language because both did. There were, as a result, contradictory opinions among the British as to whether Hindustani might be deemed to function as a *lingua franca* for the subcontinent. John Gilchrist wrote:

> This name of the country being modern, as well as the vernacular tongue in question, no other appeared so appropriate as it did to me, when I first engaged in the study and cultivation of the language. That the natives and others call it also *Hindee*, Indian, from *Hind*, . . . cannot be denied; but as this is apt to be confounded with *Hinduwee, Hindooee, Hindvee*, the derivative form from *Hindoo*, I adhere to my original opinion, that we should invariably discard all other denominations of the popular speech of this country, including the unmeaning word Moors, and substitute for them *Hindoostanee* . . . Hinduwee I have treated as the exclusive property of the Hindoos alone; and have therefore constantly applied it to the old language of India, which prevailed before the Moosulman invasion; and in fact, now constitutes among them, the basis or groundwork of the *Hindoostanee*, a comparatively recent superstructure, composed of Arabic and Persian, in which the two last may be considered in the same relation, that Latin and French bear to English: while we may justly treat the *Hinduwee* of the modern speech or *Hindoostanee*, as the Saxon of the former . . .
> (1796: 4)

However, Henry Colebrooke would declare that it was a corrupt and purely local dialect:

> Hindustani... comprises numerous dialects from the *Orduzebán*, or language of the royal camp and court, to the barbarous jargon which reciprocal mistakes have introduced among European gentlemen and their native servants. The same tongue, under its more appropriate denomination of Hindí, comprehends many dialects strictly local and provincial.
>
> (1803: 203)

Through the late eighteenth and nineteenth centuries, 'Hindustani' became the colonial *lingua franca* for all the Company's public transactions with Indians. Hindustani was seen as the one common language for the subcontinent itself. Duncan Forbes puts it this way in his 1845 grammar, *Hindustani Manual*:

> Throughout the extensive empire of India, from Cape Comorin to Kashmir, and from the Brahmaputra to the Indus, the Hindustani is the language most generally used. It consists of two dialects: that of the Musalmans, commonly called the Urdu or Rekhta, and that of the Hindus, called Hindi. The former abounds in words and phrases from the Persian and Arabic; the latter confines itself to words of native origin, or words borrowed from the Sanskrit.
>
> (1918: 1)

John Gilchrist published *A Grammar of the Hindoostanee Language* in 1796, a text that would mark the beginnings of a serious effort to understand the language so that civil and military officers serving in India could acquire it. (Gilchrist himself was adapting the work of George Hadley who had published his *Grammatical Remarks on the Practical and Vulgar Dialect of the Indostan Language, Commonly called Moors* in 1772.) Numerous such 'grammars' were produced through the nineteenth century. Part of the reason for this emphasis on language acquisition was, of course, the distrust of the native munshis and interpreters–translators. By 1801, written examinations to test proficiency in Hindustani among potential Company employees were already in place. Candidates at Haileybury were expected to translate from Hindustani into English and vice versa. In 1813

Lord Minto would declare that the acquisition of Hindustani language would:

> fit them for a more easy and perfect performance of their ordinary professional duty, and qualifying them for occasions which the Military Service frequently presents, of conducting important affairs, requiring both personal and written intercourse with Native Chiefs and Princes, qualify them also, to undertake, with great advantage to the Public, and with much honor and benefit to themselves, Political deputations and commissions, not immediately connected with their Military functions.
> (cited in Roebuck 1819)

Initial works on the Hindustani language were directed at acquiring enough linguistic proficiency as to issue orders, as Peter Friedlander has noted (2006, Steadman-Jones 2007). What Gilchrist work of 1796 does is incorporate the study of literature into the acquisition of the language, citing examples from the poetry of Mir, Daud and Sauda. But beyond the purpose of disseminating the language among the English ruling class and functionaries, the grammarians also saw their project as codifying Hindustani, purifying it and stabilizing its features. Gilchrist would speak of how 'every Hindustanee word may be uniformly and easily rendered' (3), aided of course by the very 'uniformity requisite in a Dictionary' (4). With this work, his reputation was established, and in 1800, Gilchrist was appointed Professor of Hindustani and College of Fort William, Calcutta.

In 1815 H.H. Wilson the Orientalist would praise Gilchrist's project thus:

> [He had] reduced it from the state of an unfixed, fluctuating dialect to regular permanent consistence. Before his time the Hindustani language existed only in the precarious condition of conventional use . . . The value of the article thus successfully redeemed from the operations of chance and time is unquestionable.
> (Wilson 1824: ix–x)

Thus, the documentation and 'systematization' of Hindustani might be seen as part not only of the colonial project of developing what Bernard Cohn would term 'the language of command' through the 'command of language' (1996) but also as an orientalising project. As David Lelyveld puts it, Gilchrist's aim was to 'define Hindustani as a unified language that extended over the whole of India' (195–6).

In the early twentieth century, a textbook would reiterate that to know the language is to understand the colonized native:

> To talk Hindustani, or to translate it, it is first necessary to think like a Hindustani; and such thought can only be acquired by, first constantly talking with natives and, secondly, by reading their colloquial language, the early reading lessons being written in pure colloquial language.
> (Phillott 1913: xii–xiii)

Hindustani was the *lingua franca* of the military, used by the sepoys among themselves and between sepoys and officers (Green 2009: 143). Therefore, to facilitate this communication, grammars were designed for use by Company officials and military officers. An instance of this kind of grammar would be Edward Cox's *The Regimental Moonshi* (1847), designed, as he stated, to help the English soldier and officer: 'in acquiring a knowledge of the dialect spoken by the Sepoys of that Presidency' (v) because the sepoys spoke in a 'peculiar style' (vii).

Hindustani was also the target language for the missionaries: it would enable them to reach a wider audience. With this specific aim in mind, Henry Martyn translated the New Testament into Hindustani, publishing it in 1810.

Hobson-Jobson
The term derives from the English interpretation of the chant 'Ya Hassan, Ya Hossain!' heard during the Muharram procession. Henry Yule and A.C. Burnell used it as the title of their extremely popular glossary of Anglo-Indian terms, *Hobson-Jobson: The Anglo-Indian Dictionary* (1886).

Hobson-Jobson was subtitled 'A glossary of colloquial Anglo-Indian words and phrases, and of kindred terms, etymological, historical, geographical and discursive', and proved to be more than a dictionary. In her detailed introduction to a new edition of *Hobson-Jobson*, Kate Teltscher notes the glossary's many layers: its sense of cultural superiority as well as colonial anxiety, reinforcement of imperial ideals and their subversion on another occasion, its ethnographic dimension, among others (2013). The intention, as Yule puts it, was to compile a list of 'that class of words which, not in general pertaining to the technicalities of administration, recur constantly in the daily intercourse of the English in India' (xv).

Numerous authors, including Tom Stoppard and Salman Rushdie and the Indian polymath writer Nirad C. Chaudhuri (who wrote an

Introduction to the 1994 edition of *Hobson-Jobson*), have found the work stimulating and delightful. In Stoppard's *Indian Ink*, two characters Flora and Nirad, compete to use as many *Hobson-Jobson* words as possible:

Flora: "While having **tiffin** on the **veranda** of my **bungalow** I spilled **kedgeree** on my **dungarees** and had to go to the **gymkhana** in my **pyjamas** looking like a **coolie**."

Nirad: "I was buying **chutney** in the **bazaar** when a **thug** who had escaped from the **chokey** ran amok and killed a **box-wallah** for his **loot,** creating a **hullabaloo** and landing himself in the **mulligatawny**."

The larger project of *Hobson-Jobson* was to demonstrate how Indian origin words had been a part of the English language for years. As Yule puts it in his Introduction:

> words of Indian origin have been insinuating themselves into English ever since the end of the reign of that of Elizabeth and the beginning of that of King James, when such terms as calico, chintz, and gingham had already effected a lodgement in English warehouses and shops, and were lying in wait for the entrance of English literature.
>
> (1996: xv)

Even with all its quirks and idiosyncrasies, *Hobson-Jobson* was a serious contribution to the systematization of all things colonial – whether language or customs, religion or topography. As an imperial project it imposed patterns, interpretations and prejudices over the subcontinent – for instance in its accounts of Jagannath. *Hobson-Jobson* is part of the larger project of enumeration, classification and cataloguing that made the imperial archive. Such a project as *Hobson-Jobson*, along with the numerous dictionaries, grammars, compendia, guidebooks, handbooks, maps and catalogues produced through the late eighteenth and nineteenth centuries embodies a textual control and discursive management of the colony.

Hookah

Its origins are debated, with some dating its presence to the early sixteenth century. It might have been used to smoke tobacco or something else, and was a popular apparatus in the Mughal period, especially in the homes of the wealthy. The substance was vaporized and then circulated through a water-basin and then inhaled.

The British took to the hookah as a mode of socializing with the wealthier natives. It was as a later historian of the Company would put it, 'the grand whiler away of time' in Calcutta (Carey 1906, 1: 100). William Hickey notes in his late-eighteenth-century memoirs:

> The most highly-dressed and splendid hookah was prepared for me. I tried it, but did not like it. As after several trials I still found it disagreeable, I with much gravity requested to know whether it was indispensably necessary that I should become a smoker, which was answered with equal gravity, "Undoubtedly it is, for you might as well be out of the world as out of the fashion. Here everybody uses a hookah, and it is impossible to get on without . . . have frequently heard men declare they would much rather be deprived of their dinner than their hookah".

The British also preferred glass hookahs, and cut-glass hookahs became a marker of high-fashion in Victorian England. Ornamental and ornate hookahs were manufactured by Wedgwood. Additional equipment included hookah carpets, some of which were imported into English homes from Belgium. The hookah-bearer was an elaborately dressed servant in some cases, as seen in the paintings from the times ('Hookah-bearer', 1830, in Archer 1972, plate 45).

Some of the British in India used hookahs at meal-times, although, writes Thomas Williamson in his *East India Vade-Mecum* (1810), it was more often introduced after dinner (2: 114). Indeed, Williamson claimed, the hookah was one of the luxuries of British India (along with 'shampooing', the 'snuff-box', 'the brandy-bottle') that had become 'so habitual as to plunge us into indescribable uneasiness whenever they may be out of our reach' (199). Charles Doyley devoted an entire chapter to 'A Gentleman with His Hookah-burdar, or Pipe-Bearer' in his *The European in India* (1813). Doyley claimed that the habit was 'universally retained among the Europeans' (unpaginated). Doyley also noted that the native servant, the hookah-burdar, often 'imposed on their masters the most nauseating mundungus under the high sounding title of Bilsah Tobacco!' He then offers a detailed description of the apparatus, complete with a visual representation. George Atkinson (1859) noted that Englishwomen also smoked the hookah (unpaginated).

Many Englishmen, mourns Doyley, were so addicted to the habit that they hired two hookah-burdars, for the day as well as the night. Others like Doyley saw the practice as contrary to British style and as a habit that did not do the ruling class proud. 'For a gentleman to *become a slave to his hookah* . . . it *is* beyond endurance'. The commentator claimed it was a sign of indolence and characteristic of the tropical natives and so should not be adopted by the virile, energetic English (cited in Patterson 2009: 111).

Hookah-burdar
It is from the Persian, meaning hookah-bearer. His wage, according to Doyley, was 'six to ten rupees monthly' (1813: unpaginated).

Indigo
Indigo as the source of a fabric dye was the centrepiece of investment, political policy and eventually resistance in colonial India.

Ancient Egypt was familiar with oriental indigo and its presence in the Greek and Roman worlds dates back to the second century BC. The subcontinent might have given the dye its name: *indicum* from Indies, and the Iberian word *anil* might be etymologically linked to the Sanskrit *nila*. Indigo plantations came up in the Caribbean, South and Central America and South Asia in the seventeenth century. When the Caribbean shifted to sugarcane the British decided to make India the capital of its indigo production. By the early decades of the nineteenth century, Bengal was the leader in indigo production. But to assume that the British were instrumental in bringing indigo cultivation to India would be flawed as the historian Blair Kling (1966) pointed out in an early study because local networks and production was already established before European colonization.

The demand for indigo was so high that the planters, seeking higher profits, forced local farmers to substitute food crops with indigo cultivation from the 1820s. The planter did not cultivate indigo on his own land (called 'nij', or 'own' farming) with hired labour: instead, he advanced money to peasants in the area and induced them to plant the crop (called 'raiyati' or peasant farming). Although allowed to own land after an 1837 law, very few planters actually sought to purchase land outright.

This meant the planter was under constant pressure to procure indigo and protect his investment (Kling 19). The farmers themselves made no profits, since the planters paid less than 2.5 per cent of the market price for the indigo they extracted from the farmers. Often the peasants did not, or could not, deliver the requisite quantum of raw materials, resulting in losses for the planter. A planter complained: 'a Bengali ryot very seldom keeps his engagement in anything if he can help it' (cited in Tirthankar Roy 2011: 64).

The zamindars were, expectedly, on the side of the planters. Between 1855 and 1860, production fell by nearly 25 per cent, and the principal banker, Union Bank of Calcutta, had already collapsed in 1847, leaving the planters in debt and they put further pressure on the farmers as a result. Although the Lieutenant Governor of Bengal, John Peter Grant, often ruled against special favours of the planters and sought to address petitions by farmers, things deteriorated rapidly. Earlier, Ashley Eden, joint magistrate, issued an order which stated 'since the ryotts can sow in their lands whatever crop they like, no one can without their consent and by violence sow any other crop . . . if the ryotts wish to sow indigo or anything else the policemen will see that there is no disturbance' (cited in Kling 70). Economic historians have proposed that one of the key reasons for the crisis in indigo plantation was the absence of appropriate contractual and institutional mechanisms to deal with risk, often leaving the planter with little options. Planters also had no legal redress mechanism, and therefore the rebellion was the result of the failure of the *state* (Tirthankar Roy 2011).

The peasants rebelled, refusing to take any advances for the spring sowing of 1859, in Nadia, Pabna and other districts. Village headmen often took the lead, and specific castes such as the Aguri and the chandals may have been at the forefront of the fight (Kling 85–6). Several zamindars aided the peasants, although others sided with the planters.

The rebellion was put down, with many peasants executed. However, the 'Indigo rebellion' did result in a positive outcome. In 1860 the government enacted a law that protected farmers from forced cultivation of indigo.

Prakash Kumar has argued that the plantation owners were also instrumental in pushing the frontiers of scientific knowledge. There was, he notes, a wealth of textual knowledge about methods of cultivation. 'Improvement from the planter's perspective meant increasing the yield with a higher content of color' (2012: 7). Kumar claims that such scientific developments also enabled the planter to situate himself in a global flow of knowledge and commodities. Experimentation and research into plant species and processes, he argues, spurred local knowledge production. Figures like Michel Eugene Chevreul, Edward Schunck were thus instrumental in establishing Bengal indigo as a globally respected and sought after commodity due to their emphasis on good quality dyes, made possible by refined processes of production. However, be that as it may, colonial science such as embodied in the indigo production system, cannot be delinked from the horrifically exploitative, commercial and inhuman colonial processes that constructed the plantations in the first instance.

Deenbandhu Mitra's play, *Nildarpan* (1859, translated into English by the poet Michael Madhusudan Dutt), chronicled the events and was the first major text to document the horrors of the plantation. Rev. James Long who was instrumental in getting the play printed, and who circulated it to several people in the government, was prosecuted for publishing defamatory statements by the government and for libel by the planters. In the introduction, which has been attributed to Long, he described the play as an instance of the 'annals of the poor' and 'pleads the cause of those who are the feeble' (1861: iii). The play's critique of colonial rule is visible from its very opening scene where the peasant Sadhu mourns:

> it is not yet three years since the Saheb took a lease of this place, and he has already ruined the whole village . . . Three years ago, about sixty men used to make a daily feast in the house; there were ten ploughs, and about forty or fifty oxen; as to the court-yard, it was crowded like as at the horse races; when they used to arrange the ricks of corn, it appeared, as it were, that the lotus had expanded itself on the surface of a lake bordered by sandal groves; the granary was as large as a hill; but last year the granary not being repaired. . . Because he was not allowed to plant Indigo in the rice-field, the wicked Saheb beat the Majo and Sajo Babus most severely; and how very difficult was it to get them out of his clutches; the ploughs and kine were sold, and at that crisis the two Mandals left the village.
>
> (5–6)

It depicts the threats issued by the white planters ('If you don't hear the Amin, and don't plant the Indigo within the ground marked off, then shall we throw your houses into the river Betraboti, and shall make you eat your rice in the factory godown,' 6) and the rise of peasant leaders like Nabinn Madhob as rebels. A century later, Christine Weston's novel, *Indigo* (1943), would return to the scene. Weston was the daughter of a British indigo planter, and grew up in India. The stages in the production were depicted in a set of eight visuals in *The*

Graphic (1887) and in visuals printed in the works like William Simpson's *India: Ancient and Modern* ('Indigo Factory, Bengal,' 1867) and the *Illustrated London News* ('Indigo manufacture in Tirhoot, Lower Bengal,'1869).

Jamadar
The term refers to the leader of a group of servants to the zamindar. He was in charge of the guards as well and was called upon to battle peasants should they rebel against the landlord. When the British Indian army was formed, the jamadar became a junior rank.

Jazail/juzail/jesail
It is the handmade, rather heavy and long-range Afghan gun which enabled the frontier tribes to wage efficient guerrilla warfare against the British in the nineteenth century. The jazail was often crafted from parts taken of British rifles, and indigenously modified, even decorated. Its most famous deployment was during the Anglo-Afghan wars when, during the 1842 British retreat from Kabul to Jalalabad, the Pashtuns fired at them continuously from hillocks and elevated places – one British officer alone made it back to the camp.

Years later Kipling would speak of the indignity of loss to the local jazail:

> A scrimmage in a Border Station
> A canter down some dark defile
> Two thousand pounds of education
> Drops to a ten-rupee jezail.

Jogi (see Fakir)

John Company
The East India Company was informally known as the John Company or, the Honourable John Company. Founded through Elizabeth's charter signed on 31 December 1600, it was started by a group of 218 merchants based in London. The charter stated:

> that they [the merchants], at their own adventures, costs, and charges, as well for the honour of this our realm of England, as for the increase of our navigation, and advancement of trade of merchandize, within our said realms and the dominions of the same, might adventure and set forth one or more voyages,

with convenient number of ships and pinnaces, by way of traffic and merchandize to the East Indies, in the countries and parts of Asia and Africa and to as many of the islands, ports and cities, towns and places, thereabouts, as where trade and traffic may by all likelihood be discovered, established or had; divers of which countries, and many of the islands, cities and ports, thereof, have long since been discovered by others of our subjects, albeit not frequented in trade of merchandize.

> ('Charter Granted by Queen Elizabeth, to the Governor and Company of Merchants of London, Trading into the East Indies'. From Shaw, J. *Charters Relating to the East India Company from 1600–1761.* Madras: Madras Government Press, 1887.)

James Lancaster sailed out from Woolwich in February 1601 under this charter, carrying £20,000 worth bullion, and £6,000 worth English exports. Initially the Company raised separate stocks for every voyage but by 1657 it had evolved into a permanent joint stock corporation. The round trip took anywhere up to two years. From around 1700, many of the sailors on the **East Indiamen** (the ships bound for India) were Indians, and called **lascars**.

The English East India Company, which was a late entrant into the fray, with the Dutch already fairly well established in South Asia, and the Portuguese pre-dating both by several decades. They had to engage in protracted battles with the Dutch for control over the trade. The Company ships were attacked by the Portuguese, as documented in the accounts of James Lancaster, Thomas Middleton, Nicholas Downton and others. Thomas Elkington offers a terse description of the threats faced by the Company from the Portuguese in a letter of 25 February 1614:

> You must expect to be crossed therein by the Portugal with all the force he can make; so that it shall be needful every year, to have your goods go and come in safety, to send no less strength than is sent with us, but rather more. For we see now, and is much to be doubted, that every year they will increase theirs. And whereas some think that going thus strongly provided for three or four years it may chance quite to discourage them, you are to think that those that have so long enjoyed so beneficial a trade to them will put very hard for it before they

will be thrust out, having their forces so near at hand that they do it with little or no charge in regard what you are at.

(Foster 1899, 3: 11)

With Thomas Roe's visit in 1615–19, the East India Company gained considerable leverage, with the Mughal Emperor Jahangir granting them permission to not only trade but build factories and have residences. The Company's factories multiplied in number over the next decades, and Fort William (Calcutta) and Fort St George (Madras) were created around factories. The Company negotiated trade treaties in India, but also maintained an army of its own. There were other provocations too. At Surat, where their ships landed, they were subjected to intensive customs searches including, if some of the letters are to be believed, body searches by the Mughal customs officer, Mukarrab Khan, who figures prominently in Thomas Roe's journal (*The Embassy of Sir Thomas Roe to the Court of the Great Mogul*) as a villain.

At sea their ships often encountered pirates and the vessels of the Dutch, Portuguese and later French East India Companies. The life of the factors and the early days of the Company were documented mainly as letters home, and these were later compiled by William Foster into multi-volume sets (*Letters Received by the East India Company from its Servants in the East*; the 13-volume *English Factories in India*). This was a tough life, not the least due to the enormous quantities of local liquor that several of the soldiers and factors were addicted to. The mortality rate in Bombay for instance was so high among the Company employees that the Englishman's life in India was said to be limited to 'two monsoons' (cited in Carey 1906, 1: 99. This gave Theo Wilkinson the title of his major book on the deaths of the English in India).

The Company acquired its own headquarters in Leadenhall Street in 1648. It was headed by one Governor and 24 Directors (called Court of Directors), with Thomas Smythe being the first Governor. Through the seventeenth century the Company expanded. To Surat, where a factory had been built as far back as 1612, it added Madras (Fort St George) in 1639, Bombay (Bombay Castle) in 1668 and Calcutta (Fort William) in 1690. By 1647 the company had 23 factories and 90 employees operating in India. Profits were good: 'in the year 1676, so large had these been, that every shareholder and stockholder of the old East India Company was paid a premium which doubled the stock he held', notes W.H. Carey in *The Good Old Days of Honourable John Company* (1906, 1: 25).

From the 1680s the Company's relations with the Mughals deteriorated. Skirmishes, arrests of Englishmen, embarrassing negotiations recurred through the period, with John Child, the Governor at Bombay, and responsible for much of the ill-planned moves of the Company, died in the process, a deeply unhappy Englishman in India. The Company's attacks on the native rulers were treated, rightly, by Aurangzeb as aggression and at one point ordered the arrest of Child himself. The Bengal side of the Company did not fare very well either, partly due to the tensions between William Hedges and Job Charnock jostling for power in the Hugli belt, and eventually the factors were sent away and placed under the control of the Madras branch of the Company.

A second East India Company was formed in 1698, but merged with the original one to become the United Company of Merchants of England Trading to the East Indies in 1708. The Charters were periodically renewed as India contributed more and more to the British exchequer, but the progress of trade was never easy, as John Keay (1993) and the earlier work by K.N. Chaudhuri (*The Trading World of Asia and the English East India Company, 1660–1760*, 1965) demonstrate. As early as 1760 a commentator would note that 'the whole trade of the vast peninsula of India, from the gages to the Indies, the most extensive and profitable sphere in the world' (*Annual Register* 7 [1761]: 56). Such comments were repeated elsewhere too (*Annual Register* 9 [1766]: 20, *Annual Register* 10 [1767]: 41). By 1793, India provided £500,000 annually (Bayly 1989: 120). By 1798 George Forster could declare: 'the English should no longer account themselves sojourners in this country; they are now, virtually, its lords paramount' (1798, 1: 3).

The Company's prospects and expansion were best allegorized in Spiridione Roma's *The East Offering Her Riches to Britannia* (1778), displayed in a ten by eight feet canvas in the East India House, London. Benjamin West in 1818 documented Emperor Shah Alam handing over the tax-collecting rights to the Company (1765) in a painting, *Shah Alam Conveying the Grant of the Diwani to Lord Clive, August 1765*, thereby committing to visual record a significant moment when the Company effectively became the principal political and commercial authority in India. Shah Alam, although sitting on the Emperor's raised seat, leans and bends forwards as he hands the scroll to an erect and stern-looking Clive, almost as though Alam is the supplicant.

The Company's wars in India, primarily Plassey (1757) and Buxar (1764) heralded its unstoppable expansion, except for a brief period of uncertainty during the Anglo-Mysore wars in the last decades of the eighteenth century. With stories of private wealth amassed by its officers and of widespread corruption the British government stepped in with its Regulation Act of 1773 and ensured that the Parliament would assert sovereignty over the Company. The Nabakrishna case of the 1780s, when Raja Nabkrishna 'gifted' Rs 300,000 to the Company at Hastings's behest/request and from which Hastings began to pay himself (Hastings was deeply in debt by this time). However, Nabakrishna was seeking appointment as a Company official, and so it was deemed as a bribe by Hastings's detractors. Such cases indicted the mercantile policies of the Company.

The prosecution of Warren Hastings in the British parliament from 1788 was part of this assertion of control and to stop corruption among Company servants. With the Pitts India Act of 1784 the political activities of the Company was placed directly under the Parliament, although it retained considerable freedom in its commercial activities.

The Company's corrupt practices became a byword in England. Private trading and unredeemed debts had ruined its finances. In the Ninth Report of the Select Committee published in 1783, Edmund Burke computed that the 'annual plunder of its [India's] manufactures and its produce' was approximately 'twelve hundred thousand pounds' (cited in Robins 127). Burke would state:

> From being a body concerned in Trade on their own account, and employing their servants as factors, the servants have at one stroke taken the whole trade into their own hands, on their own capital, at their own risk: and the Company are become agents and factors to them, to see by commission their goods for their profits.
>
> (cited in Robins 128)

Conservative statesmen like Burke would see the Company's activities as dishonourable for having overturned the native systems of social order in addition, of course, for being so morally corrupt. Burke accused the Company of disregarding India's ancient civilization and treating the nation as savage. In its pursuit of market dominance, Burke believed, it had abandoned all moral scruples and in the process ignored the natives' wisdom, rights and civilizational merits. Burke's views were expressed with considerable power at the impeachment of the Company's man, Warren Hastings, starting in 1788. In his opening speech – which lasted four days, and his closing address, in 1795, was nine days long, with people often paying up to £50 a seat to listen to him – Burke would indict Hastings on many counts, but it was also in effect an indictment of the Company. Burke would declare that Hastings had acted arbitrarily and then proceed on his famous accusations:

> I impeach him in the name of the Commons of Great Britain in Parliament assembled, whose parliamentary trust he has betrayed.
> I impeach him in the name of all the Commons of Great Britain, whose national character he has dishonored.
> I impeach him in the name of the people of India, whose laws, rights and liberties he has subverted; whose properties he has destroyed; whose country he has laid waste and desolate.
> I impeach him in the name and by virtue of those eternal laws of justice which he has violated.
> I impeach him in the name of human nature itself, which he has cruelly outraged, injured and oppressed, in both sexes, in every age, rank, situation, and condition of life.

As a result of these practices, the debts of the East India Company amounted to £5,393,989 in 1801. Later, through the East India Company Act (1813) and the Government of India Act (1833), the Parliament tightened its control over the Company, which lost its monopoly with the 1813 Act, and became the real ruler of the subcontinent. Company rule came to be known colloquially as Company Raj.

Through the late eighteenth and nineteenth centuries (on either side of the epochal Mutiny of 1857), there were skirmishes between the Company and tribals, local rulers in the Malabar, peasants, Marathas and Sikhs. The tightening of land taxes and monopoly extraction, the treatment of the kings were prime reasons for such upsurges (see Gough 1974 for peasant rebellions). With the overthrow of Tipu Sultan in Mysore in 1799, their biggest challenge since Plassey was over. With Tipu, Wellesley argued, 'the spirit of insubordination and contempt' among the Indian Muslims was put down forever (cited in James 2003: 65). The Company's most sustained challenge after Tipu came in 1857 when the Indian sepoys revolted, and between 1857 and 1858 the Company's existence was at stake. Having wrested back control the Company was eventually dissolved in 1873 and the British government took direct control of India.

John Company, as Nick Robins (2006) notes, was the world's first multinational corporation. It 'bridged the mercantilist world of chartered monopolies and the industrial age of corporations accountable solely to shareholders' (5). The Company created, also, the British Empire, starting off as a trading outfit and in just over 150 years establishing its political dominance. Other historians like John Keay have noted how corruption, greed, personal ambition accompanied political chaos and intrigue in the work of the 'Honourable Company' (also the title of Keay's 1994 book). Thus, instead of merely treating the Company as a well-organized corporation, historians also point to its internecine rivalries, dishonesty and personal greed as instrumental factors in crafting policy or initiating action in the subcontinent.

Juggernaut
The term is the English version of 'Jagannath' and refers not only to the Hindu god but also to the annual Jagannath festival and rituals at the temple in Puri, Odisha. Famous for its chariot festival, the temple became iconic for a wholly different set of reasons in British writings on India.

It finds mention in the fourteenth-century text of Friar Odoric and is a frequent citation in sixteenth- and seventeenth-century English travelogues on India. The descriptions focus on the giant chariot that crushes the devotees as it moves along carrying the deity. Over the course of the nineteenth century the term was used to denote any public festival, particularly of the religious kind.

Religious festivities and gatherings were suspect in British accounts, the tone for which was set in the seventeenth century. John Fryer compared the men and women dancing in religious processions to 'the Bacchanalian youths that used to revel it with Flora's strumpets in Rome' (1698: 44). The music, they believed, was mere noise and the celebratory/joyous festivity was grotesque and disorderly. Thomas Herbert writes of a false religion such as Hinduism in whose religious processions 'poor[e] wretched bodies [are] miserably crusht in pieces' by the 'ponderousness of the idoll' (1634: 192). Thomas Bowrey describes in detail how the fanatics hurled themselves under the wheels of the chariot carrying the idol, before terming it 'diabolical' (1997: 17–18). The entire spectacle is described as grotesque and monstrous, and the bodily regimen (over-dressed, dishevelled – for example, fakirs), behaviour (singing and dancing) were seen as indicative of a deformed social order itself. The French physician Francois Bernier described the chariot as 'a chariot of hellish triumph' (Bernier 1826, vol II: 6). Claudius Buchanan, a missionary attended the 1806 festival, called it detailed the wretched state of the devotees, the dirt and the possibilities of disease (Buchanan 1817: 281–284). Later, in studies of Indian architecture, such as James Fergusson's *Picturesque Illustration of Ancient Architecture in Hindustan* (1848), there would paintings of the procession, showing the packed crowds. The English saw the entire ritual as a symbol of not only the depravity of the belief system but also of the cruelty of the practices that sacrificed devotees to the god. Thus in *Jane Eyre* a character is described as 'worse than many a little heathen who says its prayers to Brahma and kneels before Juggernaut' (Bronte: 56).

By the nineteenth century the ritual of Jagannath's chariot procession acquired the sense of 'the Juggernaut: a massive, inexorable force that crushes everything in its path', as the *Oxford Dictionary* defined it. This was partly the effect of the coverage of stampedes during the procession. In 1822 a stampede killed about 30 people, and the *Asiatic Journal* of 1824 gave considerable attention to the tragedy.

The Juggernaut also became a symbol of the dangers of crowds in India, especially after the coverage of stampedes and instances of disease. In the nineteenth century the occasion of the festival was utilized by the British government to institute laws about crowds and sanitation, arguing that the crowded setting was unhygienic and so the movement of people needed to be regulated. Thus at the 1866 International Sanitation Conference in Constantinople the participants argued that Europe was at threat from cholera originating at primarily Hindu religious gatherings such as Jagannath, but also from the Muslim Hajj. Described in terms echoing the seventeenth century, these commentators, and later ones like W.W. Hunter (who described Jagannath thus in 1872: 'every year . . . this homicidal enterprise massacres six times more men than Plassey') treated it as the space of sensual excess. This stance enabled the British government to bring in medical and sanitary measures, ostensibly to control epidemics like cholera coming out of Jagannath, but was in actuality an attack on Hinduism itself (Arnold 1993: 187–9). Establishing a link between religion, crowds and disease, all embodied in the Puri festival, the government was able to put into place rigorous measures of surveillance and crowd control.

Indian festivals were the object of considerable curiosity for the British, evidenced by the commissioning of paintings by artists like Sewak Ram of the Holi, Harihar Kshetra festivals, the Muslim wedding procession and others (see Archer 1972, plates 37, 38).

Jungle

It means uncultivated and wild growth and is derived from Persian and other languages. Nathaniel Halhed in his *A Code of Gentoo Laws* (1776) defines 'land waste for five years' as 'jungle' which, according to the *OED*, is the first use of the word in English. However, at least one scholar notes that an MD thesis submitted to Edinburgh University used it eight years prior to this, with the Sanskrit Anglicized (Goulding 2006). Soon after, in 1783, Edmund Burke used the word as well, aligning it with 'deserts'.

The sense of uncultivated and uninhabited land was central to the British imagining of the wilder parts of the subcontinent, although, as was eventually proved, there were tribals living in most of the jungles.

The jungle begins to be a matter of some concern from the late eighteenth century. It was unproductive land, to begin with. In 1798, George Forster passing through Jumah describes 'a thick gloomy forest, tenanted only by the beasts of the field, skirts it on the eastern side; and on the other, an uncultivated flat, over-run with low wood' (1798, 1: 196). The British government was concerned about land that had no economic value – an ideology that came over from England where numerous commentators such as Arthur Young, William Godwin and others saw uncultivated land as a 'public nuisance' (Young 1768: 145).

One move to address this concern was to transform the forest areas specific types of forests, first embodied in the Forests Act of 1865 but proceeding through later Acts as well through the nineteenth century. With these Acts, the tribals and other communities living in the forests lost their way of life because the forest land was redefined as 'government' land and they were 'encroachers'. A decade earlier, teak from forests had been made government property and its sale was regulated by the Forests Charter of 1855. Dietrich Brandis was appointed the first Inspector General of Forests in 1856 and he began the process of classifying the trees in the Indian jungles. Forests were 'reserved', 'protected' or 'village'. In the first category the government asserted total control over the area because these were the most commercially viable forests. 'Protected forests' were more accessible, but not entirely. Fuelwood gathering, grazing and such activities of the local communities were permitted but controlled in here. 'Village forests' were areas meant for use by the people of the region. Richard Grove has examined how so-called ecological and conservation policies of the colonial state not only established the state's control over the land, but also profoundly affected the lives of people who lived with/in the forest areas (1990: 17). Grove notes that, besides the need for control, colonial conservation policies were the result of an interest in limiting environmental degradation that could have deleterious effects on the state's economy.

The second move was to make the forest/jungle a space for legitimate recreation and sport. By the mid-nineteenth century the Indian jungle was much sought after – as a fine place for sport. Richard Grove has argued that aesthetic concerns informed colonial forest conservation policies, in so far as the colonials wished for Edens and tropical paradises (18). Regulating the forest area ensured that the savage, threatening and limitless forest was now mapped and organized for utilitarian purposes. Questing for places that were not mapped and converted into tourist attractions, the English man, and sometimes the Englishwoman, sought the forest as a space of unsullied purity. It has been argued that in an age when 'unknown' places were reducing in number, the English sought an 'extreme exotic' (Nayar 2008: 132–68). This was the jungle. It became the space where the Englishman asserted his masculinity fighting the wild (although they were very often accompanied by an entire team of native beaters that drove the animals into shooting distance). The Englishman voluntarily embraced risk in the subcontinent's jungles, and thereby demonstrated, ostensibly, a true English spirit.

Kedgeree/cutcherry

It is derived from the Hindi 'khichri', a dish made of legumes and rice cooked together, with vegetables and sometimes nuts. The British in India apparently liked the dish so much that they adopted it when they went back home. John Fryer describes it as 'cutcherry' in his 1698 travelogue, but added that the Indians 'grow fat' on this (Fryer: 81).

Older recipes for the dish included fish along with the rice as well. In 1845 Eliza Acton is believed to have devised a version with eggs in it.

Khansamah

Khansamah is the native servant in charge of the kitchen, especially procurement of supplies. British homes in the colony gave enormous powers to the khansamah, where he was the head servant. Some texts describe him as the 'butler' of the Anglo-Indian household.

The khansamah, it was suspected by many a memsahib, made a neat profit on purchases. The anonymously authored *The Englishwoman in India* (1864) has this to say about the family butler:

> This domestic is the most expensive and riseless of any, and one which I never advise being engaged, as a good 'Head Boy'

answers the purpose far better. The butler, par excellence, generally confines his business to walking to and from the bazaar to make purchases for the house, on which he gets as large a profit as he possibly can. He is supposed to write the accounts and take the entire charge of the whole establishment, superintending the other servants, the more menial of whom he dismisses and engages at will, this obtaining great influence over them. He is a necessary portion of a mess or club, and in some very large establishments, where constant parties are given . . .
(42–3)

According to the best-selling nineteenth-century domestic manual, Flora Annie Steel and Grace Gardiner's *The Complete Indian Housekeeper and Cook* (1888), where again the khansamah is called a 'housekeeper and head waiter', he is described as a 'useless servant' (54–5).

The khansamah's authority was unquestionable, often even by the memsahibs and sahibs of the house. In Rudyard Kipling's 'My Own True Ghost Story' the narrator describes the khansamah as being 'as ancient as the bungalow' (McGivering: n.p.). Kipling adds:

> He either chatters senilely, or falls into the long trances of age. In both moods he is useless. If you get angry with him, he refers to some Sahib dead and buried these thirty years, and says that when he was in that Sahib's service not a khansamah in the Province could touch him. Then he jabbers and mows and trembles and fidgets among the dishes, and you repent of your irritation.

The khansamah employed in dak bungalows and clubs was often the repertoire of stories about previous residents and their doings. In the above story, Mangal Khan, the dak bungalow's khansamah, tells the narrator of the Englishman who died at the billiards table (the narrator hears billiards being played, apparently in the uninhabited house – and assumes they are ghosts of former players):

> It is long ago, but I remember that one Sahib, a fat man and always angry, was playing here one night, and he said to me:— 'Mangal Khan, brandy-pani do,' and I filled the glass, and he bent over the table to strike, and his head fell lower and lower till it hit the table, and his spectacles came off, and when we – the Sahibs and I myself – ran to lift him he was dead.

Khitmutgar/kitmutgar

A term mostly used in the Bengal Presidency, it signified a servant who waited at the dining table. His position was lower than the khunsumah in the social order of the English home in the colony. The duties were detailed in Steel and Gardiner's *Complete Indian Housekeeper and Cook* (73–9).

The khitmutgar is described thus:

> a curious mixture of virtues and vices. As a rule, he is a quick, quiet waiter, and well up in all dining-room duties; but in the pantry and scullery his dirt and slovenliness are simply inconceivable to the new-comer in India.
>
> (Steel and Gardiner 73)

Flora Annie Steel and Grace Gardiner, advising the memsahib to keep a sharp eye on the servants in the household, open their book (chapter titled, 'Duties of the Mistress') with the khidmutgar's behaviour as an illustration of servant behaviour:

> They [the memsahibs] never go into their kitchens, for the simple reason that their appetite for breakfast might be marred by seeing the khitmutgar using his toes as an efficient toast-rack (fact), or their desire for dinner weakened by seeing the soup strained through a greasy turban.
>
> (1–2)

The khitmutgar's salary was between Rs 9 and 10 a month. There was no need for more than one khitmutgar in a house, advised Steel and Gardiner:

> Above all, nothing is more insensate than the multiplication of khitmutgars. If a man cannot wait on six people, he is not worth keeping as a table attendant.
>
> (37)

The khitmutgar had a habit of being over-enthusiastic at the dining table and this was unacceptable, the authors advise:

> When there is a large party at breakfast, it greatly conduces to the familiar comfort of all to have small sugar basins and cream or milk jugs at intervals down the table, and there

should be at least two plates of butter and toast. In regard to the former, the khitmutgar should be generally discouraged from making it the medium for a display of his powers in plastic art; it is doubtless gratifying to observe such yearning after beauty, even in butter, but it is suggestive of too much handling to be pleasant.

(46)

Lac

It is the resinous secretion, mostly from *kerria lacca* insects, used for various purposes such as wood finish, cosmetic and dyes.

Documents from the nineteenth-century link 'lac' with 'lacquering'. Here is a report from 1835:

> The manner of colouring turnery toys furniture and other articles made of wood is a very pretty art and it deserves particular attention as it is not known in Europe this art is called lacquering The small insect called Coccus Lacca deposits a substance on the branches of certain trees which is called Lac; this substance goes through several processes which are well known; the toy men purchase it in the state of Shell Lac; then the operator first holds a piece of bamboo over a charcoal fire; when the bamboo is heated he sticks some pieces of Shell Lac upon it; and when these are sufficiently warmed other pieces are put upon them until there is as much as he can conveniently manage having thus softened a sufficient quantity he takes it off the bamboo and mixes the colouring ingredients with it by kneading them together working them well together with his hand and hammer; when the whole of them are perfectly combined together, he draws out the whole in the form of a stick of sealing wax; the colouring materials used are vermilion from China and from Europe, sulphurat of arsenic, indigo and lakee which is extracted from lac. These materials are combined so as to produce ten different colours in addition to the natural colour of lac. Some other ingredient may be used in the process of colouring lac black The turner takes a piece of kooreya wood hammers it into the end of his lathe and when fashioned he presses a piece of coloured lac against it by friction he generates a degree of heat which softens the lac and causes it to adhere to the wood when the article is sufficiently covered with lac he polishes it in his lathe by means of

the leaf of the *Pandanus Odoratissimus*, stripped of its thorns this leaf is pressed against the article. When tent poles and such large articles are lacquered a fire is burned beneath them to soften the lac but in lacquering Patna toys this is never done ... Lac is also formed into bracelets for Hindoo women. The lac for bracelets is first heated then by means of a wooden instrument which is also used by the raj mistry in compounding mortar for floors it is rolled out into the form of a bracelet this is finished off on another instrument.

('The Machinery Used in Patna and Thiroot', 1835: 154–5)

George Watt in his *A Dictionary of the Economic Products of India* (1889) offered a detailed account of the mode of growth of the 'lac insect' and listed the trees on which it may be found (2014, 2: 409–10).

In the late nineteenth century, lac was in demand by American and European gun manufacturers, as insulating varnish and a wood preservative. Large firms were contracted to purchase lac from forest dwellers. This was a shift in the nature of the economy around lac because previously lac was procured from forest dwellers by local artisans and this entry of the internationally hired large firm altered the nature of the forest dweller-artisan link (Archana Prasad 1994, cited in Jeffrey et al).

Reports of lac cultivation in other Asian colonies were also compiled – for instance in works like Dorothy Norris' *A Report on the State of Lac Cultivation and the General State of the Lac Industry in Burma* (1931) – indicating a major international interest in the product.

Lascars

From the Persian 'lashkar' meaning a camp or unit of the army, the word 'lascar' came to signify sailors and seamen in the European lexicon during the colonial era. John Fryer in the seventeenth century used the word spelt 'luscar' to suggest 'soldier' (as opposed to the lascar, or seaman). Eventually it was used to describe native seamen in the service of the Company.

Lascars were hired, at very low wages, at all the major Presidency towns and served on Company ships to England. Their wages, depending on their rank, were detailed in an early study, Dinkar Desai's *Maritime Labour in India* (1940). They were hired as gangs rather than as individuals, and many of them made multiple trips to Britain. In an account from 1903, W.H. Hood notes how lascars from the Punjab were better than those from Sylhet in Assam (10–11). There was a hierarchy within lascars – serangs, tindals, casabs, paanwallah – and were variously assigned to the engine room, the saloon or the decks. Visual representations of the lascars appeared in *The Graphic* (2 Feb. 1889) and other places in England. William Mulready's 'Train Up a Child In the Way He Should Go, and When He Grows Up He will Not Depart from It' depicted an English boy, looking worriedly at three lascars, huddled in blankets, giving them alms at the urging of the two Englishwomen accompanying him. As Michael Fisher notes in *Counterflows to Colonialism*, it suggests that the English boy is being instructed to overcome his fear of aliens and show charity to even them. It further suggests, according to Fisher, that the English *expected* to meet destitute lascars in their country (147).

Lascars received extremely harsh treatment. The problem of ill-treatment was already so acute in the seventeenth century that in 1783 regulations were passed for the proper treatment of Indian servants including lascars. It became mandatory for lascars embarking on voyages them to carry an indemnity bond so that they would not be left destitute and becoming chargeable to the Company – a measure that was not, Rozina Visram notes, very effective (Visram 2002: 11). They were given severely cramped quarters on the ship (European seamen got better space) and many died on the voyage according to a study conducted in 1922 (Home 1922). Home published, almost yearly, mortality statistics of European and Indian sailors in the respected *Lancet* through the late 1920s and 1930s as well. Beriberi was a common affliction due to the poor diet the lascars were supplied with. Beatings, being tied on to the decks, humiliations were commonplace (Joseph Salter in his 1896 work, *The East in the West*, mentions some of these). The 1883 Indian Merchant Shipping Act prescribed a list of provisions due to the scale of the nutrition problem of sailors and diets/provisions were listed in the *Gazette of India* in 1931. As Ravi Ahuja puts it: 'the maritime labour market of the nineteenth and twentieth centuries was structured into a rigidly racist hierarchy with South Asians at its bottom' (2006: 112).

Due to protests from the British seamen, it was ruled that ships sailing to the East Indies could only hire lascars when 'ascertained that a sufficient number of British seamen cannot be procured for the crew'. The same statute, as recorded in *A Digest of the Public General Statutes* (1822), stated that

> No ship so licensed [to trade with the East Indies] shall be permitted to clear out from any port . . . until the owner or

captain shall have given security by bond . . . for the maintenance and conveyance back to India, or for the conveyance to England maintenance while in England and conveyance back to India, of such lascars or Asiatic seamen.

(224)

Discipline on the ships was deemed to be very important in order to keep the lascars in order. W.H. Hood however notes that the lascars were 'amenable to ordinary discipline . . . they just do their work and attend to their duty decently' (43). Hood attributes this to the rather primitive 'Eastern' mind when he writes: 'chipping or scrapping iron or steel, painting, scrubbing or cleaning, holystoning decks but cleaning, always cleaning, does not require a very high standard of intelligence to perform it' (43). Consequently, a 'much more efficient state of discipline prevails on the lascar-manned steamer than can ever be hoped for on similar vessels manned by the ordinary type of European crews' (49).

Once their voyage ended in England, they were left to fend for themselves and hired out their labour for menial work in Liverpool, Brighton and other port towns. They represented their case to the Crown in England, as Michael Fisher has demonstrated in *Counterflows to Colonialism* (2004), when they were left destitute, demanding that the Company takes responsibility for them. There was an occasional attempt made to document statistics about the lascars, as ordered by the British Parliament, with some like Captain Hughes claiming that of the 10,000–12,000 lascars arriving in England in 1855, 3,000–3,600 were Indians (Visram 1986: 52. Also, see Fisher 2006 for statistics on lascars in the 1760–1850 period).

Frequent illnesses due to the cold weather and poor food meant that the lascars had a very bad time in England. Eventually a home for their stay was built on the West India Dock Road, Limehouse, London by the Society for the Protection of Asian Sailors in the 1850s. Some of the lascars who stayed longer periods took on English wives and integrated into English society. Later there were Indian seafarer unions formed in the late nineteenth century, and commentators like G. Balachandran propose that they evolved 'collective and individual strategies of survival' due to 'their very neglect by the state and their rather fraught relations with the trade union movement in Europe' which paradoxically 'endowed them with a degree of autonomy' (2003, unpaginated).

Lascars represent the first wave of South Asian immigrants to England and Europe (Visram 1986). They developed their own lexicon and vocabulary, called by the Europeans 'Lascari-Bat' (lascar-talk), and documented in a volume *Lascari-Bat: A Collection of Sentences Used in the Daily Routine of a Modern Passenger Ship* by A.L. Valentini (1892).

Heathcliff is described as a 'little Lascar or an American or Spanish castaway' in *Wuthering Heights* due to his dark looks and uncertain origins – suggesting that he is an outsider, as lascars were.

Lat sahib

The subcontinent's version of 'Lord Sahib', it was originally used as a term for the Governor General of India but began to be extended to Lieutenant Generals as well. But there were 'cadres' to the designation as well. The Mulki Lat Sahib, or Lord of All the Land, was the Governor General or Viceroy. The Jungi Lat Sahib was the Commander-in-Chief, the Lord of War. Then there was the Punjab Lat Sahib, the Lieutenant Governor of Punjab.

Lock Hospital

Originally founded in England in the 1740s to treat sexually transmitted diseases, these began to be set up in India from around the 1820s. Prostitutes diagnosed with such diseases were confined to such hospitals, but the incidents of diseases did not go down in number (Ballhatchet 1980). There were civil and military Lock Hospitals, with the latter outnumbering the former.

The anxiety over prostitution was in fact a military anxiety: that British soldiers and sailors who arrived at the ports were visiting these 'unregulated' prostitutes and catching illnesses (Tambe 2009: 35. Also Levine 2003). There was thus an intrinsic connection between the various Army Sanitary Commissions, the legislations, the military and the medical organizations around the question of Indian women's sexuality, even as it regulated British soldier bodies. By the 1820s, well before the Contagious Diseases Acts (1864, 1868, and against which the formidable Josephine Butler campaigned), the Bengal Presidency reported over 4,000 admissions across its 18 hospitals. *Annual Reports* from the various hospitals across the subcontinent recorded 'number treated', 'average daily sick' and 'average daily stay in hospital'. It should be noted that Lock Hospitals were meant not to provide medical care for general population of Indian women but for Indian prostitutes. Occasionally the reports would also admit that poverty, famine and starvation drove women into prostitution. For instance, the *Annual Report on the Lock Hospitals of the Madras Presidency, for the year 1877* stated:

> The increase in the numbers of treated in Military Lock Hospitals appears to have been due largely to the pressure of the famine, under which numbers of starving women, many of them seriously diseased, flocked into and practised prostitution in several of the large cantonments and towns. The returns for civil institutions are not complete, but so far as the Presidency town is concerned there is sufficient evidence to show that the numbers of prostitutes and consequent prevalence of venereal diseases, were largely increased by the terrible necessities of the famine. In one Native Regiment, quartered at Madras in the neighbourhood of a large relief-camp, the admissions from venereal diseases were so numerous as to attract attention, and the explanation given was that numbers of starving women who had immigrated from the districts were practising prostitution and that many of them were diseased.
> (1878: 4)

The Lock Hospitals were part of the larger project of legislating sexual behaviour and were extremely coercive in nature, with rigidly enforced diet plans included. Doctors were mandated to examine the prostitutes and issue bills of health as part of this process of sanitizing sex. Yet, it was not medicine alone that determined the attitudes of the British government towards prostitution. The evangelical movement influenced their attitudes and moral reform was very much an agenda for the various commissions investigating prostitution. Prostitution was a proof of Indian barbarity itself and had to be rooted out (Tambe 13). Other commentators have noted a clear binary in the representation of prostitutes in medical reports emanating from commissions and such hospitals. The prostitutes were either villains who inflicted the disease of British soldiers or they were hapless victims. The latter, it was underscored, required the Lock Hospital (Wald 2014: 70).

Loot

It is from the Hindi/Urdu *lut* meaning plunder and the Sanskrit *lotra* meaning rob, to take by force. The 1788 Stockdale's *Vocabulary* lists the word to mean 'plunder' and 'pillage', according to *Hobson-Jobson*.

Maa-baap

A short-hand term for the paternalistic benevolence that supposedly marked the colonial master's relations with the colonized subjects, 'maa-baap' was meant to indicate 'I am your father and mother'. The white man was in the role of the maa-baap, and the native subject in the role of the child.

The term served many purposes. First, it established the relation as being one of authority: parent and child. Second, it infantilized the colonized subject, and thereby indicated that s/he is incapable of agency, will and autonomy. With this, the discourse of 'maa-baap' was able to institute the colonial master as the person in charge, since children require parental support. Third, it erased the violence built into the colonial master–subject relations by proposing, instead, a benevolent protectionism. The parent was in charge but was also a kind parent as keen on civilizing the child as disciplining it. Fourth, the maa-baap role the British assigned to themselves implied a moral superiority of the white race that then both encouraged and necessitated taking on the 'white man's burden'.

The maa-baap ideology was not unique to India but was embedded in a larger ideological movement in England itself, that of 'improvement' and benevolent paternalism. Benevolent paternalism and improvement were inspired by the Clapham Sect and the Abolitionist movement and was a constituent of a global humanitarian regime (Lester 2000, 2012). While not strictly within the maa-baap mould, the paternalism of the Abolitionist movement reflects similar ideological positions. For instance, there were two stereotypes of the white plantation owner in the Caribbean in the literature of Abolitionism: the cruel master or the benevolent one. In Maria Edgeworth's short story 'The Grateful Negro' (1804) the master Edwards earns his slave, Caesar's loyalty through his benevolence. In James Grainger's long poem, *Sugar-cane* (1764) he writes:

> In time, a numerous gang of sturdy slaves,
> Well-fed, well-cloath'd, all emulous to gain
> Their master's smile, who treated them like men,
> Blacken'd his Cane-lands: which with vast increase,
> Beyond the wish of avarice, paid his toil.
>   (unpaginated, http://mith.umd.edu/eada/html/
>   display.php?docs =grainger_sugarcane.xml)

This was particularly the ideology that informed the **sahibs** in India. Lord Elphinstone would summarize it well in his grandiose and dramatic statement: 'the most desirable death for us to die should be . . . in the improvement of the natives' (cited in Cotton 1892: 185-6).

There were, of course, some contradictions and conflicts within this role essayed by the British in India. Often the burden became too much to bear and works that critique the Empire are sharply questioning of this assumption of moral superiority. Colonel Layton in Paul Scott's *A Division of the Spoils* presents himself as the maa-baap to the soldiers under his command, but as his daughter Sarah Layton admits, the 'effort of living up to it had become too much for him' (344). In the first volume of this Quartet, *The Jewel in the Crown*, Edwina Crane, the missionary woman, fails to protect her loyal assistant, Mr Chaudhuri:

> 'I can't help it,' she said, as if to him, when he lay bloody and limp and inhuman in the place she had dragged him to. 'There's nothing I can do, nothing, nothing,' and turned away and began to walk with long unsteady strides through the rain, past the blazing car, toward Mayapore. As she walked she kept saying, 'Nothing I can do. Nothing. Nothing.'
> (1978: 69)

Then there was the contradiction in the view of the natives as well. On the one hand, benevolent paternalism assumed that under the white man's tutelage the colonized subject, with potential for improvement, would be civilized. On the other hand, they also treated the natives as innocent children incapable of such a change (Dube 2004: 38-9).

Memsahib

The white woman in India was often designated as the 'memsahib'. The memsahib was portrayed in many different ways. The memsahib's role in the structure of the Empire in India has attracted considerable controversy and discussion. Whether the memsahib endorsed the imperial values or whether she utilized the colonial setting to acquire a measure of freedom and agency otherwise denied her in England (as a woman) is an ongoing debate.

One type of memsahib found in colonial writings was the frivolous and snobbish Englishwoman in the colony. She spent her time attending parties, writing letters home to England and doing little else. She was overtly racist, and for the better part of the stay in India ignored the natives except those she needed to live her life (such as the servants around her house). Many of these women eventually became melancholic due to the sheer boredom, according to commentators from the time. Flora Annie Steel in her autobiography, *The Garden of Fidelity*, declared: 'the majority of European women in India have nothing to do' (1929: 122). Decades earlier G.O. Trevelyan had painted the portrait of such a bored Englishwoman in India:

> The ladies, poor things, come in for all the disagreeables of up-country life. Without plenty of work, India is unbearable. That alone can stave off languor and a depth of ennui of which a person who has never left Europe can form no conception. In a climate which keeps every one within doors from eight in the morning till five in the evening, it is, humanly speaking, impossible to make sufficient occupation for yourself, if it does not come to you in the way of business. After a prolonged absence from home, reviews and newspapers become uninteresting. Good novels are limited in number, and it is too much to expect that a lady should read history and poetry for six hours every day. What well-regulated female can dress an object in a society of a dozen people, who know her rank to a title, and her income to a pice; or music, when her audience consists of a Punkah-wallah and a Portuguese Ayah? Some ladies, as a matter of conscience, go very closely into the details of household affairs; but after a time they come to the conclusion that it is better to allow the servants to cheat within a certain margin, for the sake of peace and quietness; for cheat they will, do what you may. Oh! The dreariness of that hour in the middle of the long day, when the children are asleep, and your husband has gone to tiffin with the judge, and the book-club has nothing but Latham's "Nationalities of Europe" ... and the English post has come in yesterday, with nothing but a letter from your old governess, congratulating you for being settled among the associations of the Mahommedan conquerors of India, and asking you to take some notice of her nephew, who is in the office of the Accountant-General of Bombay. It is very up-hill work for a lady out here to keep up her spirits and pluck, and her interest in general subjects. The race-week, the visit to her sister in the Punjab, the hope of being ordered down to Calcutta, the reminiscences of the sick-leave, and the anticipations of the furlough, are the consolations of a life which none but a very brave or

a very stupid woman can endure long without suffering in mind, health, and tournure. If a lady becomes dowdy, it is all up to her; and the temptations to dowdiness in the Moffusil cannot be well exaggerated.

(1992 [1866]: 120)

The memsahib, especially of the first variety, was often instructed to treat her home as an adjunct to the Empire project. Flora Annie Steel and Grace Gardiner announced in their 1888 manual: 'an Indian household can no more be governed peacefully, without dignity and prestige, than an Indian Empire' (Steel and Gardiner 1909: 11). Consequently she sought to assert stringent control over the servants in her households – and there were numerous servants, with the number reaching a hundred in the wealthier English colonial home – in what has been termed an 'imperial discourse of domesticity' (George 1993–94, Blunt 1999: 426, Joseph 2004). We see this in discourse manifest in Steel and Gardiner's comment/advice:

> The first duty of a mistress is, of course, to be able to give intelligible orders to her servants . . . The next duty is obviously to insist on her orders being carried out . . . The Indian servant is a child in everything save age, and should be treated as a child: that is to say, kindly, but with great firmness.
>
> (Steel and Gardiner 1909: 2–3)

This ideological construction of the memsahib as a necessary embodiment of imperial ideals was also partly driven by the felt need of ensuring the Englishwoman's virtue in the colony. It was deemed to be the Englishwoman's responsibility to retain English honour. This meant a careful attention to the duties of a wife and mother. Her clothes, dancing skills, social etiquette, ability to organize proper meals, organize festivities for children, behave with a consciousness of rank and hierarchy were under scrutiny in the social sphere of the colony, in clubs, in the 'At Homes' and at the various parties. Further, as commentators have noted, the Englishwoman had a carefully regulated sexuality, in contrast with the supposedly hypersexual and sensual Indian one (Grewal 1996: 45). That is, for the sanctity of the English home in the colony the Englishwoman focused on her wifely and motherly duties and not on her own sexuality. Novels, such as that of Alice Perrin, often depicted as object lesson, the 'disorderly Memsahib' (Indrani Sen's apposite term, 2002), unable to assert a 'proper' English femininity, regulate her servants or her sexuality and be true to the imperial grand design (Nayar 2012).

The memsahib served also to illustrate another key point. The status of women in any society was deemed to be an index of its civilization and development. In imperial discourse it was implicit that while the Europeans knew how to 'treat' women, Indians and other races did not, and therefore were barbarians. This binary was a myth. Philippa Levine writes: 'that the position of women in white societies at this juncture was perhaps less than ideal for women was not an issue; it was 'primitives' who apparently failed to respect proper womanhood and not the British' (2004: 7).

The second dominant stereotype of the memsahib was the school teacher, nurse, missionary, doctor memsahib: earnest, working to ameliorate the conditions of her poor native sisters. She was self-sacrificing and took her responsibility towards the colonial subjects seriously, often encountering considerable hardships in her chosen career in India. This second type of memsahib was embodied in Mary Carpenter, Annette Ackroyd, Florence Nightingale and others whose work involved collaborating with native patrons in the cause of women's health or education in the colony. Several of these women, as Vron Ware notes, were sceptical and suspicious of British paternalism, and stayed outside the network of missionaries, and were mortally offended by the racism of fellow Englishwomen (Ware 1992). Annette Ackroyd records how several of the memsahibs had never spoken to the natives. She comments:

> How these sweet and feminine souls, whose empathy is so tender and sensibilities so acute, can be so destitute, not only of humanity, but of simple courtesy and consideration of the feelings of others, is a problem I cannot pretend to solve.
> (cited in Barr 1978: 163)

The women who went out thus into the outposts of the Empire disturbed the trope of the 'protected' and chaste femininity and domesticity but also signalled a rejection of the English male's protector role.

Many English writers blamed the Englishwomen for muddying the imperial project. Forster claims in his 1924 novel *A Passage to India* that the Englishmen would have made greater efforts to socialize with the Indian guests but are 'prevented from doing so by their womenfolk whom they had to attend, provide with tea, advise about dogs, etc' (1970: 46).

Moor

The term originally referred to the Muslims of the Iberian peninsula, to Muslims in general and then to people from northern Africa. In the Medieval and Renaissance periods, 'Moors', 'Mahometans', 'blackmoors', and even 'Indians' were used as synonyms. Alden Vaughan and Virginia Vaughan point out in Elizabethan England the 'black moor' was mostly associated with sub-Saharan Africa (1997). Some further classification was put in place to describe 'tawny' Moors from northern Africa and 'blackamoor' from sub-Saharan Africa (30, n. 31. Also Matar 2000).

The Europeans began to use the term derived from the Portuguese 'Mouros' to describe Muslims of the subcontinent but also of Ceylon and South-East Asia. Thus the term was synonymously used with 'Mohammedans' and had no specific national or regional connotation. John Fryer's (1698) travelogue makes this elision of 'Moor' with 'Muslims' very clear: 'Their crew were all Moors (by which word hereafter must be meant those of the Mahometan faith')' (Fryer: 24).

Mufti/mufty

In Persian it signified an Islamic scholar, often attached, like the **qazi** and the faujdar, to the criminal court in order to help administer Muslim law.

When it entered English around the early nineteenth century, it signified civil or 'plain clothes' army men, as *Hobson-Jobson* defines it while tracing this sense of the word back to Moliere. For *Hobson-Jobson* this was: dressing-gown, slippers and a smoking-cap. It simply signified 'not in uniform' which is the sense in which it is used even now to describe, for instance, police or army personnel in civil dress.

Munshi

It meant both teacher and secretary, although the original term referred to a man of learning, especially in the languages. In British India, the Persian teacher was the munshi, who also trained people in Persian letters. In southern India too, the munshi was a Tamizh teacher. At some point, secretaries, clerks and writers were called munshis.

Charles Doyley's *The European in India* (1813) offered a detailed account of the munshi. First describing him as a 'linguist', Doyley writes:

> This profession is not invariably filled by the Mussulmans, though there are very few instances of Hindoos being Moonshees . . . The learning and writing of the Moonshees is extremely confined. Writing a fair hand, an acquaintance with

> the provincial anomalies, and a readiness at reading the multiplicity of manuscripts which are consigned to them for explanation, ad which are sometimes difficult to decipher as many of our nearly-illegible English writings; added to a copious string of quotations from the Koran, and a general acquaintance with the very few books extant in India in the Persian language, mostly the lives of great men, or the poems of Hafiz, &c may be said to comprise the requisites for being classed among the sages of the East.

Doyley noted that the munshi was considered the 'head of servants', but was paid a low wage. He saw them as neither 'so respectable, or so well informed' (unpaginated).

The munshis were native sources of information. They prepared surveys of areas for their colonial masters and provided local histories (Bayly 1999: 226–7).

The relationship between the British employer and the munshi was a fraught one, as recent commentators have noted. Often the British author relying upon the munshi for translations of native works found the munshi either unequal to the task or wilfully subversive. John Gilchrist, for instance, in the preface to his *A Dictionary, English and Hindoostanee* (1787–90) complained about his greedy munshis who contributed to the project's delay and escalating costs (cited in Ogborn 234). William Jones, Francis Wilford and numerous others were also constantly in pursuit of the trustworthy pundit and munshi (Raj 2001).

Munshis, in Bengal and in the Madras Presidency, were expected to follow a modern grammar of their respective languages, but often ended up, as Bhavani Raman demonstrates, with a polyglot Tamizh minus the grammar (101). This significantly altered the munshi's, and the pundit's, embeddedness in his own cultural and intellectual milieu. As C.A. Bayly has argued, the original pundits and munshis were secure in their own intellectual fields and served as native informants to the Empire from this position. But by 1840s, the 'new generation of munshis had been subjected to European disciplines' with new modes of diary-writing and empirical descriptions (1999: 373). This considerably altered their role in the information hierarchy of the Empire, often colluding but sometimes subverting the information exchange intended by their colonial masters (373).

Queen Victoria's trusted Muslim attendant, taken from India to serve her in England, Hafiz Mohammed Abdul Karim, was given the title 'Munshi' by the Queen.

Muslin

The name derives from 'Maisolos', the port of Masulipatnam in southern India, from where this fabric was traded between the subcontinent and Europe. The term is used to describe an assorted set of fabrics though. For instance Marco Polo describes 'cloths of gold and silk' as 'Mosolins', but attributed it to Mosul in present-day Iraq. The material was exported to Persia and Turkey as well.

With increased trade more of the muslin and other cottons arrived in England through the seventeenth century. But even as these were being imported and consumed an economic and cultural anxiety around Indian materials, and Oriental products in general, began to be articulated in England. A petition by 'fann-makers' to the House of Commons pleaded that the importing of 'fanns and sticks, as well as silk and callicoes' should be stopped in order to protect England's own manufactures (Anon, *The Case of Fann-makers*, 1670, np).

Bengal was a leading producer of the fabric. William Bolts claims in his 1772 work, *Considerations on Indian Affairs* that there was an even finer variety of muslin manufactured in Dacca for the exclusive use of the Emperor's seraglio, 'a piece of which cost 4.00 rupees, or 5.ol sterling', and 'if spread on wet grass to have been scarcely visible' (206).

The British from the 1750s began to restrict the independent trade out of Bengal and monopolized the export of muslin and other cloth. Eventually, Britain began importing its own industry-manufactured cotton as well, thus more or less ruining the market for the more expensive Bengal muslin and cotton cloth. By the end of the eighteenth century, Britain had become a global leader in cotton textile production. In 1820, states a report, a dealer in Dacca was unable to supply a Chinese buyer the kind of muslin cloth asked for, and concludes: 'thus the art of making the very fine muslin fabrics, has perished under the infamous commercial tyranny of the British rule' (434). This skill, the author states, was such that they 'could remove an entire thread from a piece of muslin, and replace it by one of finer texture' (433). By 1840 the muslin market was in ruins, as one report in the *Asiatic Journal* on the 'Commercial Intercourse with India' debate at East India House of 22 December 1842 details:

> The cotton market had been nearly annihilated. From £1,400,000 per annum it had dwindled down to £2000 . . . The muslins and cambrics of India were not now in request . . . a mercantile firm was now selling India muslin, which five or six years ago was worth from 40s to 50s., for 10s a piece.
>
> (4)

The report goes on to indict the 'unequal duties' on English goods that ruined the India muslin trade: 3½ per cent for English products imported into India and 10 per cent duties on India cottons imported into England (4).

It was also noted that the wealthier natives in India exhibited a penchant for luxurious English products. In the House of Commons' Minutes of Evidence Taken before the Committee of the Whole House, and the Select Committee, on the Affairs of the East India Company (1813), natives 'purchase[d] articles of luxury, such as broad-cloths, watches' (37). Hence the committee asks:

> Are you able to state whether the present mode of supplying, and the amount of supply of English and European articles sent to India, has been sufficient or more than sufficient to supply the demands of the natives?
>
> (57)

Nabobs

> Clime, colour, feature, in my bosom find
> The friend to all
> Why rob the Indians and not call it theft?

The principal character involved in this 'theft' that Richard Clarke in his satirical poem, *The Nabobs* (1773) is describing, is a species of Englishman, the nabob. A derivation of the Hindi 'nawab', this termed describes an entire category of Englishmen that emerged around the mid- to late eighteenth century in India. It may have come into being first to describe Robert Clive, who made enough wealth in India, both legitimately and otherwise, as to return home to both flaunt it and continue his lavish lifestyle among his countrymen (before, of course, he committed suicide). The other candidate for the title of the first nabob is, at least in Michael Edwardes's book, Warren Hastings.

The nabobs were usually from the middle and working classes in England, with little prospects there, who came out to India and were employed in the East India Company. Some of them acquired wealth as adventurers and mercenaries. The nabobs were in India principally for their own good and were therefore not averse to cheating their employer, the EIC, in order to make a profit. Many in fact abandoned Company employment to work exclusively on trade contracts, on commissions. Very often they took to native costumes and frequented native women – sometimes acquiring them as 'bibis'. With wealth came considerable pomp, and the former merchants now began to call themselves 'gentlemen', or its Indian equivalent, 'nabobs'. Their lavish lifestyles, large houses, numerous servants, heavy drinking and gambling – many drove themselves into debt – made them immediately unpopular with both the 'respectable' English merchants and factors, and the Indians. The nabobs were known for their greed, but also for their arrogance and utter want of any kind of responsibility toward India (which would characterize the latter category, the sahibs).

Some nabobs like Thomas Hickey and George Thomas would pretend to be local rajahs as well. In fact George Thomas who acquired a large territory in the present Haryana region declared his own 'capital', populated 'his' city with five to six thousand people and crafted laws for the place himself (*The Military Memoirs of George Thomas*, 1803), and came to be called a 'Rajah'.

Samuel Foote's play *The Nabob* (1768) satirized their lifestyle, greed and unscrupulous dealings. H.F. Thompson's *The Intrigues of a Nabob* (1780) exposed the Hastings regime, and his personal life. Richard Clarke's poem cited above was subtitled 'The Asiatic Plunderers', leaving no doubts about what he thought of the entire class. When they returned to England as 'old Indians', they were characterized by, writes W.H. Carey in *The Good Old Days of the Honourable John Company* (1906), 'excessive wealth, diseased livers, a repulsive querulousness of manner, and a luxurious way of life' (1: 105).

Nautch/nautch-girl

Swaying slowly she quits her station.
All one silken undulation,
Past the rows of swarthy faces . . .
She winds her snaky wreathings to the droning of the hymns;
Till the truth is lost in seeming,
And our spirits fall a-dreaming, . . .

This is Trego Webb writing about the Indian 'nautch-girl' in the nineteenth century. But the first accounts of the Indian dancing girl can be found in the seventeenth-century travelogues of Thomas Herbert, John Fryer (who called them 'strumpets'), John Ovington and others. Derived from the Hindi word 'naach', the 'nautch' was a major social event in the life of the Englishman, especially of the lower class of soldiery, in India. The early accounts are unanimous in declaring the performance ugly, noisy and unbearable. Some, like Bishop Heber in the 1820s, believed that because the nautch-girl was 'ugly, huddled up in huge bundles' she would be 'dull and insipid' to the Englishmen (Heber 1829, II: 105). This was so patently not the case that there were even attempts to frame laws prohibiting Englishmen from visiting these performances because they came to be seen as sexually charged and therefore morally corrupting. Many therefore would have agreed with James Forbes's account of them in *Oriental Memoirs* (1813): 'They are extremely delicate in their person, soft and regular in their features, with a form of perfect symmetry, and although dedicated from infancy to this profession, they in general preserve a decency and modesty in their demeanour, which is more likely to allure . . .' (Forbes 1834, Vol I: 61). One Englishman recorded how many nautch-girls had retired from the cities and retreated into cantonments (Captain Williamson, *Costumes and Customs of Modern India*, 1813). Paintings by Charles Doyley (*The European in India*, 1813) depict the popularity of the nautches. Several of these nautches began to be performed in the Englishman's home from the 1780s. Paintings such as 'Mahadaji Scindia Entertaining Two European Officers to a Nautch' (1820, reproduced in Archer 1972, plate 59) suggest that it was a popular way of passing time for the British, and a major means of socializing with the ruling classes for the Indian aristocracy.

The nautch-girl was central to the British imagining of India as a place more than likely to seduce the unprepared Englishman, as can be seen in Forbes's account. Like the Arab-Turkish harem and the seraglio, the Indian nautch was the space of dangerous unbridled sexuality. Doyley in fact classifies the nautch-girls across the country:

> The women of the Upper Provinces are generally much fairer than those of Bengal Proper. They also wear more ornaments; they dance with more precision; though not, in general, with such wanton gestures as the latter.
>
> (unpaginated)

The comparison to the snake, the traditional tempter in Webb's poem (to be repeated in texts like Geoffrey Mundy's *Pen and Pencil Sketches*, 1832), is no coincidence.

The nautch-girl represents one of the widely circulating stereotypes of Indian women, the others being: the vulnerable woman (epitomized by the widow/*sati*), the scheming Indian queen/princess, the assertive upper-class Indian woman, and the docile bibi, and the crusading evangelical Indian woman.

Opium

Opium's centrality to the British social and literary imagination – beside the economy – is of course best documented in the life and work of the poet Samuel Taylor Coleridge and the essayist, Thomas de Quincey, the author of *Confessions of an English Opium-Eater*. Other poets such as Percy Shelley and George Crabbe were also users of opium and its derivatives, and critics have long been interested in the link of opiates and the English Romantic poets of the 1790–1830 period (Abrams 1934, Milligan 1995, Singer 2009).

Opium becomes a key product in the East India Company (EIC) economy from the last decades of the eighteenth century. Growing poppy in the Bengal province, the EIC began exporting opium to China, although China's emperors had tried to shut down imports due to increasing addiction among their citizens. (Artists like Thomas Allom depicted the addicts in opium saloons in Canton.) Further, the Chinese regulations about foreigners – whom they called barbarians – entering their territory were very strict: prohibitions on foreign vessels entering the Pearl River, prohibitions on traders bringing their wives and families, a fixed number of servants, trade through licensed merchants only, among others.

The profits from the opium exports were channelized into buying expensive Chinese products such as silk and tea, for which there was a massive demand in England. In 1773, the Bengal government assumed a monopoly on the production and sale of opium in Bengal and transformed Indian opium into a commodity of exchange. By the 1820s, opium replaced cotton as the most profitable EIC's Indian export to China.

By the 1830s nearly 40,000 chests of opium were exported into China. Islands in the Canton Bay area were sites of transactions, with the active collusion of some Chinese officials (Collis 1968: 23), during the course of which the content of the chests were referred to as 'foreign mud'. Parsi traders and businessmen from the Bombay region were part of the network and greatly benefited from the opium trade. Initially the missionaries in India supported or quietly endorsed the opium trade, in the interests of the Empire and British profits, although towards the end of the nineteenth century, the missionaries would be at the forefront of the opposition to opium exports from India.

Commentators puzzling over the missionary silence on the opium trade in the early nineteenth century propose that this was because 'they did not witness the widespread consumption of the drug or see up close the deleterious personal and social effects of widespread addiction' (Miller and Stanczak 2009: 338).

The EIC used private traders, who in turn used smugglers, to get the opium into China. Matters were not helped by the behaviour of the English in Canton and other places: many of them mocked the Chinese authorities, and did not consider even the officials – such as Commissioner Lin who ordered the foreigners to surrender the opium in 1839, and destroyed about 20,000 chests of opium – as worthy of respect. Lord Napier's appointment (1834) worsened matters. Ignorant of the edicts and regulations, Napier, whose designation as an officer and not a trader automatically prohibited him from entering China without the permission of the Emperor, decided to stay in Canton. The resulting tensions were the immediate trigger for the conflict.

The Chinese Qing dynasty made attempts to stop the trade, resulting in two rounds of armed conflicts, first with England (1839–42) and later with an England–France alliance (1856–60). The Chinese lost both, and the restrictions on importing opium had to be scrapped. The trade continued until 1907 when a treaty was signed between China and the British government in India to stop exports. The exports finally stopped in 1917.

The opium trade resulted in the first Parsi diaspora outside India: in China. According to one study, between 1828 and 1848, there were 40 to 45 Parsi residents in Canton. Parsi communities were documented in Canton, Amoy and Shanghai, and the first Parsi burial ground outside India was built in Macao in 1829 (Palsetia 2008: 653).

With mounting pressure from reformist and missionary groups to ban the opium trade, the British government appointed a Royal Commission on Opium. The commission amassed a wealth of testimonies and accounts (723 witnesses, of whom 466 were Indians) in 1894 in order to launch a sustained attack on the consumption of opium in India, by Indians. As John Richards has pointed out (2002), the consumption of opium for medicinal and other reasons was socially and culturally acceptable in India society, and the British critiques of this practice was a form of cultural colonization. Indian witnesses who were called to testify often reiterated the for social advantages and necessity of using opium. One stated:

> If people of my caste men who take opium and I, who take it, do not get it excepting as a medicine, then our habit and character would be changed for the worse. We would go mad. We shall lose all power of distinguishing good from bad. Our health would be entirely shattered. We shall be bereft of the power of all work. The social custom that prevails among us

of receiving our friends with opium would not only be interfered with, but would be entirely abolished.
(Royal Commission on Opium, *Minutes of Evidence taken before the Royal Commission on Opium*, 1894, 4: 390)

A few witnesses noted that in other countries people consumed liquor for the same reasons as they, the Indians, used opium. A prohibition on opium, argued one witness, would suggest that the 'government wanted us [Indians] to take to liquors', leading to serious social consequences for the consumer because, in some Indian castes, anybody who consumes liquor is 'outcast' (418).

As the British government sought to make economic and cultural interventions around the subject of opium cultivation and consumption the commission was also wary of the ramifications. The report stated in no uncertain terms: 'prohibition would beyond all doubt create the very greatest discontent' (403). The commission recommended compensation, region and district-wise, to cultivators and traders for losses incurred due to the ban on opium in India.

The final *Report* of the commission, published in 1895, took the position that opium consumption in India was akin to the Western world's alcohol consumption (as stated by the witness cited above) and was also prescribed and consumed for medicinal reasons, and that the anti-opium tirade by the Chinese was exclusively based on commercial concerns over monopoly rather than for social or ethical reasons. The *Report* stated:

> we find it proved beyond reasonable doubt that the prevalence of the use of opium is founded, first, on the universal tendency opium amongst mankind to take some form of stimulant with which to comfort or distract themselves, and, secondly, on the wide-spread popular belief in the medical or quasimedical efficacy of the drug.
> (Royal Commission on Opium, *Final Report of the Royal Commission on Opium*, 1895, 6: 16)

It argued:

> Our conclusions, therefore, are that the use of opium among the people of India in British' Provinces is, as a rule, a moderate

use, and that excess is exceptional. Moderation, no doubt, is a relative term, and its limits may vary largely in the case of individual consumers. In some localities, also, and among certain classes of the community, there may be a tendency towards excess that is not found elsewhere. But, looking to broad results, we are satisfied that the general use of opium, which may properly be described as moderate, is not attended by injurious consequences. In many parts of the country the number of those who take opium constitutes a very small proportion of the entire population, and we have no hesitation in saying that no extended physical and moral degradation is caused by the habit.

(19)

At the end of the deliberations the *Report* concluded:

It has not been shown to be necessary, Prohibition or to be demanded by the people, that the growth of the poppy and manufacture and sale of opium in British India should be prohibited except for medical purposes . . . The prohibition of the growth of the poppy and the manufacture and sale of opium in British India . . . would inflict a very heavy loss of public revenue on the Government and people of India . . . We find no evidence of extensive moral or physical degradation from its use.

(95–7)

Amitav Ghosh's *Ibis* Trilogy offers an extensive fictional account of the opium trade with China, while David Mitchell's *Ghostwritten* mocks the English for accusing the Chinese of xenophobia when the latter objected to the Company plying its poisons in Canton.

Padre

In British India it was the term adopted to designate the military chaplain (Heathcote 128). *Hobson-Jobson* notes that it was used to describe both native and European priests.

The first English priest in India was Father Thomas Stephens, who came to be known as Padre Stephens in Goa, where he arrived in 1579 as a Society of Jesus priest. An unusual padre, he learnt Marathi and Konkani and published a grammar of Konkani in Portuguese but is better known for his epic poem *Krista Purana* (*The Life of Christ*). His letter to his father appeared in Richard Hakluyt's *Principal Navigations, Voyages, Traffiques and Discoveries of the English Nation* (1599) and reprinted in Courtenay Locke's *The First Englishmen in India* (1930).

The Court of Directors that ran the East India Company ensured that every English voyage, fort, garrison and factory had a chaplain. There were, as a result, hundreds of chaplains through the 250 years of the Company (O'Connor 2012: 1–2). The first chaplain appointed for a voyage by the Court of Directors was Thomas Pulleyn. Later ones, like Edward Terry who accompanied Thomas Roe to the court of the Mughal Emperor Jahangir, wrote detailed accounts of their stay in the East Indies (1655).

Later, the army chaplain was usually selected for the job by the Royal Army Chaplains Department, established in 1796. They were only Anglican priests initially, and later Roman Catholics, Presbyterians and Methodists were also selected for the job across the British Empire. Those hired by this Department were in the pay of the British army. But other than this category of the padre there were also civilian clergymen who catered to the needs of the army in India. Michael Snape notes that several of these padres, especially the Roman Catholic ones, were not British but Italian, Portuguese, French and German, and there was a continual demand for English-speaking ones (12).

The padres were instrumental not only in spreading the Christian gospel but were actively involved in dismantling what they saw as the superstition-ridden idolatrous Hindu religion. Several served as teachers too.

The term was also appropriated to describe Muslim priests who served the spiritual needs of the native sepoys in the British Army, for instance, Afzal Shah who was called the 'Muslim padri' of the Contingents of the Nizam's Cavalry stationed at Bolarum, Hanamkonda and other places in the Hyderabad region in the 1830s (Green 2009: 39–40).

Pagoda (architecture)

Mostly Buddhist places of worship in East Asia, the pagodas became synonymous with Hindu temples in British, and other European, writings on India. Jan van Huygen Linschoten the Dutch traveller used it in his *Itinerario* of 1596.

We see the word occurring with increasing frequency in William Bruton, John Ovington, John Fryer and other seventeenth-century travellers. William Bruton describes the pagoda at Jagannath as the 'mirror of all wickedness and idolatory' (1638). John Fryer speaks of the darkness of the 'pagods' in Madras, the 'obscene images' and 'monstrous effigies' carved on the walls (Fryer: 39). Other pagods, he notes, have ancient scriptures or 'Holy Writ' of the 'Gentu language' inscribed on them (Fryer: 44). The pagoda in India becomes the symbol of Hindu superstition. Every traveller notes the darkness inside the pagoda's sanctum sanctorum, and reads it as an index of the darkness in Hinduism itself. Fryer writes: 'the work [Hindu temple] is inimitably durable, the biggest closed up with arches continually shut . . . admitting neither light nor air' (39).

Writers like Robert Southey represented the pagodas as sites of licentious behaviour. For instance in his narrative poem *The Curse of Kehama*, Southey in a footnote writes:

> Every pagoda has a band of these young syrens, whose business, on great festivals, is to dance in public before the idol, to sing hymns in his honour, and in private to enrich the treasury of that pagoda with the wages of prostitution.
> (Southey 1810: 352)

The pagodas, like all other aspects of the tropical zone, were symbols of the degenerate Indian/Hindu. Tim Fulford's comment on Southey's Kehama sums up the colonial scene of the pagoda: 'not just ornamental exotic landscapes . . . but as real places in which occurred religious rites that featured sex and sacrifice' and cites the following passage from the poem:

> Within the temple, on his golden throne
> Reclined, Kehama lies,
> Watching with steady eyes
> The perfumed light that, burning bright,
> Metes out the passing hours.
> On either hand his eunuchs stand,
> Freshening with fans of peacock-plumes the air,
> Which, redolent of all rich gums and flowers,
> Seems, overcharged with sweets, to stagnate there.
> Lo! the time-taper's flame, ascending slow,
> Creeps up its coil toward the fated line;
> Kehama rises and goes forth,
> And from the altar, ready where it lies,
> He takes the axe of sacrifice.
> (Fulford 2013: 194)

Besides these extensive accounts of pagodas as symbols of Indian/ Hindu degeneration that circulate in English travelogues from the seventeenth century and are 'imported' (as Fulford terms it in the above essay) into English writings, the pagoda also enters English culture through a different route: architectural appropriation.

From the early decades of the eighteenth-century England began to display an enhanced interest in chinoiserie (David Porter 1999, 2002). William Temple introduced the Chinese principle of *sharawadgi* (artful disorder), in an essay on gardening (1692). William Chambers, who lived in China for two years in the mid-eighteenth century, in his *Dissertation on Oriental Gardening* (1772) offered detailed illustrations and examples of the Chinese garden, drawing upon his earlier 'On the Art of Laying Out Gardens Among the Chinese' (1757). The cumulative effect of these texts and accounts of the Chinese gardens was that the wealthier English houses installed pagodas in their gardens. The Kew Gardens acquired, in 1760, a House of Confucius and a ten-storey pagoda, thanks to Chambers's influence. Horace Walpole at his famous Strawberry Hill home considered giving it a Chinese style, complete with a pagoda, an idea he later abandoned in favour of the Gothic. The pagoda was inserted into a quasi-fantasy architecture much of which, as Porter notes in his works, was closer to the Gothic, thereby generating a truly hybrid, if questionable (according to Walpole) aesthetic mode of landscaping. Other Chinese structures such as bridges and pavilions were also built in the gardens.

The pagodas in the English garden were also constitutive of a medieval revival. Further, the incorporation of these architecture designs from an entirely different, and distant, culture became a signifier of the cosmopolitan tastes of the English lord or gentleman. It was also a mode of bringing the exotic home and might be read as a form of aesthetic colonialization of the world, primarily as a method of establishing the English's ability assimilate into their landscape the world itself.

The Chinese garden of Kublai Khan, first described for European readers by the Venetian Marco Polo, would be extolled as a near-utopian place in Coleridge's 'Kubla Khan' (1797).

Pagoda (currency)

A coin in southern India, usually of gold, but also of silver on occasion. The Portuguese were using the term by the time the English arrived in India. Later the French and English Companies also minted the coins. In the seventeenth-century travelogues maintained by the

British, they enumerated the local currency their values John Fryer noted, for instance, that 32 fanams make a pagod.

Pandy/pandies

The term came into circulation after the 1857 uprisings to refer to the Indian sepoy in the British Army. It derived from 'Mangal Pandey', who was one of the first documented rebels in 1857, having fired shots at his English officers at Barrackpore. Mangal Pandey was executed, and his last name was taken up as a synonym for the native sepoy but also as a signifier of treachery, sedition and betrayal.

The treacherous pandy becomes the antithesis of the infantilized, vulnerable and easy-to-discipline native of the earlier stereotypes. In the course of the uprisings this infantilized native, who saw the English as his 'maa-baap' had risen against his 'parents', killed them and violated them in unimaginable ways.

With the uprisings, the British attitude toward the Indian sepoys, or pandies, took several forms. The most dominant one was of revenge. Driven to fury and anguish by tales of the sepoys' cruelties toward their fellow Englishmen, particularly women and children, the English officer and soldier swore revenge. Fred Roberts could think of nothing but 'giving the Pandies a damn good thrashing' in his *Letters Written during the Indian Mutiny* (1924). W.H. Russell the American correspondent in India during the uprising records how he heard officers speaking of 'potting pandies and polishing off niggers' in *My Diary in India* (1859).

Destroying the treacherous pandy was seen as an act of restoration of English pride and national character. In his eyewitness account, *Up among the Pandies*, Vivian Dering Majendie (1859) notes how the uprising and the pandies had to be put down ruthlessly because England and not just its empire was at stake:

> A crisis to meet which England must brace every nerve, strain every energy, and put out the right arm of her strength; her power was trembling in the balance, her Indian empire hung upon a thread, which one false move might sever. The occasion, indeed, was awful, but England was equal to it. Expeditiously were the measures for the defence of her Eastern empire commenced, steadily were those measures continued . . .
> (Majendie 1859: 3)

The pandies were 'fiends', a term invoked throughout the Mutiny narratives by various Englishmen and women. They were represented as 'possessed' and 'diabolical', as Christopher Herbert's recent work on Mutiny discourses in England demonstrates (2008). Hence executing and massacring the pandies was no longer either sinful or illegal. Such discourses of course reinstated the older colonial stereotype of the irrational Indian, where the pandy acted not out of a keen political sense of outrage (at being subordinated to the Englishman in his, native, land) but because he was 'possessed'. This move evacuated the Indian soldier's political beliefs, consigning him to the sole status of a volatile, out-of-control beast.

Majendie also observes, with considerable consternation, that back in England, the public has not seen the English retributive moves as a form of justice at all. Majendie writes:

> With no little astonishment, as we read speeches and leading articles, did we behold the respective positions of Sepoy and Englishman reversed, the former being the martyrs now, the latter the persecutors. Misguided officers and soldiers who had been inwardly congratulating themselves that they had established a sort of claim upon the gratitude of their country, by their services in India – and by this had been cheered up all along, through heat, sickness, and hardships – suddenly discovered, on reading the record of proceedings at Exeter Hall, and elsewhere, that it was all a mistake; and that they were, by certain sets in England, looked upon, individually, as something between a cannibal and a grand inquisitor. One unfortunate who, not anticipating this revulsion of public feeling, and who, when the cry of 'no quarter' was echoing far and wide through England, had written a little letter home, stating with much satisfaction that he had killed several Sepoys, was astonished to find by return of mail that he was a monster, and not the least bit of a hero. In fact, we were told that 'Jack Pandy' was not half so bad a fellow after all, and we really had been a little too hard on him.

Pigsticking
>There's bliss in the scholar's love, my boys,
>In wine and golden store, my boys,
>But the joys of the whole do not thrill the soul
>Like the rush of the charging boar, my boys.
>   (Baden-Powell 1889: 191)

It was also called hog hunting or boar hunt and was believed to be a great test of character and endurance: 'perhaps no diversion requires more coolness and judgment, than hog-hunting' (Williamson 1819, 1: 30). The hunter used the lance or spear and chased the pig or boar down on a fast horse.

Native princes and rulers hosted the British hunter and the hunt was, as commentators have noted, an essential form of social interaction between rulers and ruled even as underscored the Englishman's domination of the Indian landscape. The hunt was a symbol of the white race's supremacy in the colony (MacKenzie 1988, Mangan 1992, McKenzie 2000, McDevitt 2004, Pablo Mukherjee 2005). Tent Clubs were established in various stations to facilitate pigsticking, and drew up their rules for the sport (Baden-Powell 1889: 200–1).

It was also, according to Baden-Powell in his 1889 manual on pigsticking, an excellent means for the newcomer officer to know his territory of operations and a way of meeting the natives:

> On becoming a pigsticker the pursuit of sport will take the young 'civilian' to covers in all corners of his district; he will of necessity be brought into personal contact with all classes of natives of his district at unexpected times, and differently than when on his periodical and ceremonious tours of inspection; he will see for himself the state of crops, irrigation, cattle, etc., etc.; and, if a successful sportsman, he will win by his prowess a standing in the estimation of all native classes higher than any that could be obtained by a stay-at-home 'clerk-in-an-office young man'.
>
> (5)

Typically, native beaters with their drums would drive the hogs out of the cane fields and shrubs for the horse-mounted sahib to hunt them down. The beaters were given instructions about their line of march. Thomas Williamson's *Oriental Field Sports* (1819) suggests: 'the beaters should not be more than five or six feet distant from each other, else the hogs will frequently turn back, and rush through the intervals' (21). Williamson offered suggestions on chasing a hog across different kinds of terrain, the exact spot where the spear must enter the hog's body, the length, weight and other dimensions of the spear to be used, and others. He also advised the English hunter not to rely on the natives in moments of crisis: 'were he to depend on the exertions of the natives, he would stand but a bad chance: as they, in general, secure themselves by flight, wherever a hog shews the least inclination to pursue' (35).

The hunt therefore also served to illustrate the differences between English and Indian character. Writes Baden-Powell:

> Every out-of-the-way performance on the part of an Englishman in field sports is regarded by the natives of Hindustan with a stunned wonder and admiration; and even by Shikaris and jungle tribes as indicating a proper prowess in the dominant race.
>
> (1889: 6)

The boar, warned Baden-Powell, was 'cunning' (67–8) in a chapter titled 'Powers of the Pig', and thereby implies that the hunt is also a battle of wits between man and animal.

The Kadir Cup was a tournament for pigsticking (1874 onwards), but there were others such as the Meerut and Bheema cup as well.

Pindari/pindaree

It is a community classified as hereditary bandits (akin to the robber-killers, thugs). They were originally protected by the Maratha rulers, but after the destruction of the Maratha empires they were hunted down by the British. The Pindari Wars of 1817–18 effectively destroyed their power in the Maratha-Gwalior region.

The Pindaris were mostly Muslim, but later other communities also joined the army of Pindaris. They had been attached to Mughal armies and later to the Marathas. After battle, they were allowed to loot and plunder the conquered city, camp and enemy army.

Thomas Medwin, Shelley's cousin and biographer, who served in India and was part of the action against the Pindaris in the 1817–18 wars, wrote 'The Pindarees' (1821) in which he grouped Gorkhas, Arabs, Banjaras into the nomadic category of 'Pindarees'. Medwin romanticized the Pindaris as not just plunderers but as rebels who resist the law. The British in response had to take recourse to extreme savagery and forget the rules of war, as Nigel Leask points out in his reading of the poem (1996: 70).

Medwin represents the Pindaris as blood-thirsty, rapacious savages:

> 'Tis nature's ordinance – man preys on man!
> Then why should we reverse the general plan'.

> Call us Pindarees! Kossaks! to the strong,
> All that the weak protect not, should belong.
> (1821: 59)

There is also the suggestion, as in the case of colonial thugi representations, of madness, religious ecstasy and drug-induced delirium in the behaviour of the Pindaris. Medwin writes:

> 'Tis riot all in that disordered route;
> Loud shrieks succeed to every joyous shout;
> Frenzied, and like a bacchanalian train,
> They smear their garments with the Huldee's stain,
> Spring forward – dance, vault wildly from the ground;
> Or wheel in dizzying mazes round and round.
> Join hands; in multitudinous acclaim,
> Heri Hera! invoking Vishnu's name
> (60)

Oswald the Englishman is of course the hero of the tale. He rescues Seta the Indian woman from bandits (he is described as 'round which her form/Had clung for refuge, sheltering from the storm', 78) and later pursues the Pindaris.

Polo

It is believed to have originated in India, but with equivalents in ancient Persia and Turkey. Historians of the sport have tracked instances and evidence in India, such as goal posts, to the seventeenth century (Laffaye 2009). A 1904 account, T.F. Dale's *Polo: Past and Present*, declares polo to be 'the most ancient of games', adding, 'all our best games are derived from it, and cricket, golf, hockey, and the national Irish game of hurling are all descendants of polo'. (1). Dale also claims that 'the English game was in advance of the Indian one in science and tactics at first', a point he reiterates later (33, 249), thus establishing racial superiority in the field of sport as well. But Dale also admits:

> In actual skill at the game the best American players are in front of ail except the English first-class players, and I might add, the best native players in India, who would, I should imagine, if they could play on anything like equal terms, prove stronger even than our best English teams.
> (261)

Horace Laffaye believes the British office Major Joseph Scherer first discovered polo being played in the Cachar region of Assam, although it was a popular sport played in the Manipur region well before this period (10–11). Frederik Drew documented its presence in Gilgit and Baltistan around the same time as Scherer in Manipur and Assam (Parkes 2005: 63).

It acquired popularity on par with pigsticking and hunting in British India and was played on assigned days of the week (56–7) and became a regimental sport. Protective headgear was introduced (60). The British often played it with Indian princes and local rulers, thus marking a major social process. *Baily's Magazine* reported in 1875 that 'polo has been played in India by both European officers and native irregular cavalry for the last thirty years' (cited in Laffaye 2009: 13). Charles Johnson Payne's (Snaffles) lithograph *Polo: The Game of Sahibs and Rajahs* depicted Indians and Englishmen on the polo grounds.

Senior officers could afford to maintain more ponies and so were better at their game than younger men who could not afford more than one pony, which they used to regular work and for polo (Allen 1976: 133–4). Numerous tracts on the maintenance of horses were published from the latter decades of the nineteenth century.

Critical commentaries note how an indigenous sport was appropriated by the colonial race, inserted into the imperial system, its rules and structure codified in Europe – mainly the Hurlingham Association Rules of 1876 – and then the 'sophisticated canon of civilizing rules . . . were ultimately re-imposed upon a now-primitivized and peripheralized indigenous game' (Parkes 62–3). In other words, polo was reinvented by the imperial regime and 'modernized' to distinguish it from the supposedly more chaotic indigenous version, as another instance of the civilizational mission.

Various polo associations were formed and some teams, like the Golkonda team of the Nizam of Hyderabad and the Alwar team were popular. Princely houses such as Jaipur, Patiala, Hyderabad, Alwar were keen purveyors of the sport. Tournaments were organized around the country, and the Indian Polo Association (founded in 1891) was instrumental in drawing up the rules of the sport in India (printed as chapter 18 in Dale's history of the sport).

In the 1880s polo was threatened by the widespread popularity of cricket. Ramachandra Guha has noted how Indian cricket players were often complaining about how the polo players were constantly battling for the same grounds as the native cricketers. It became a battle, Guha writes, between native cricket and European polo (1998).

KEYWORDS

POSH
While not strictly an Anglo-Indian word, the term derives from a colonial context. 'POSH', now signifying luxury and style, is an acronym: port out, starboard home. This was a reference to portside cabins on ships traveling out of England toward India and the subcontinent and starboard cabins on the voyage from India to England. These cabins were away from the sunny side when the ships voyaged along these directions, and hence were more comfortable, and expensive. From this arrangement of expensive, relatively cooler cabins on the long passage to and from England, emerged the signifier of luxury, style and wealth.

The Peninsular & Oriental (P&O) liners, the oldest shipping company to serve the England–India route, were the most popular ships for the voyage to and fro India. 'POSH' came to be associated with the P&O line as well.

Presidency
The British organized the subcontinent into first Presidency Towns and later Presidencies: Bombay (capital: Bombay), Bengal (capital: Calcutta) and Madras (capital: Madras). These were the administrative units of the subcontinent. The Afghan region did not have a Presidency and was instead designated a 'Province', the North West Frontier Province.

Later regions annexed by the Company but not governed by the existing rules and ordinances of the East India Company were 'Non-Regulation Provinces'.

Punkah/punkah-wallah
The bungalows and offices had large fans, or punkahs, that required able-bodied young men to pull them continuously, with the aid of a rope that led outside the room. 'Punkahs' date back to the ancient world. From a hand-held fan to a large, swinging model operated by a pulley mechanism, the punkah has evolved considerably. In British India, the punkah was integral to the unbearably hot accommodation and offices of the sahibs. H.E. Busteed in *Echoes from Old Calcutta* (1888) claims that 'the hanging punkah came in between 1784 and 1790' (128).

Extensive descriptions of the punkah and the punkah-wallah may be found in the key text of imperial domesticity, Steel and Gardiner's *The Complete Indian Housekeeper* (1888). They write:

> Punkahs in most stations are required all the year round during the day, but from 1st November to 1st April may be

dispensed with at night. Two pullers are generally required for night work. The commonest plan, however, is to arrange a contract with a family, say for Rs. 10 a month.

(1909: 32)

Here is a detailed account of the device from Steel and Gardiner:

> punkahs are generally put up in Northern India about the beginning of April. The cloth-covered frames supplied by the landlord of the house are usually whitewashed, and after several coats the lime is sure to come off in flakes and get into your eyes. This is an evil only to be mitigated by having the frames well scraped. The Bombay and Bengal punkahs consist often of a bar of polished wood, from which the fringe hangs. This is prettier and cleaner, but it hardly gives so much wind as the broad, flat frame. Sometimes you meet with wooden panelled frames. These are best; but failing this, and if the whitewash nuisance be great, it will be found wiser to re-cover the frames with cotton dyed to match your room. The frill can be made pretty in a thousand ways. It will not cost much. There is nothing more difficult than to judge the height at which a punkah should be hung. Strictly speaking, it is always too high or too low; in other words, it either scrapes your head or leaves you perspiring. In fact, at its best it is an instrument of torture. On the other hand, it appears to please the coolie who pulls it. The squeaking of a punkah at night is very distracting, but can generally be cured by black lead or oil. The latter, however, is apt to smell. Leather thongs for pulling are dearer to begin with, but more satisfactory than ropes; nothing is more maddening than to have to get up and splice the latter in the middle of the night. A towel pinned on at night to the punkah fringe makes its sweep greater.
>
> (206)

The punkah-wallah was a key servant in households and offices that lacked electricity. Steel and Gardiner call the punkah-wallah the 'punkah-coolie' and assign their salary at Rs 5 per month (31). They were, if Steel and Gardiner are to be believed, 'very dear' to find (36). But the punkah-wallah was also, they suggest, quite lazy:

> In regard to punkahs, in the writer's opinion they are comparatively of little use except to keep away mosquitoes, or when

sleeping on the roof. At mealtimes they are a necessity. But they are too intermittent a palliative to be satisfactory. The presence of a punkah rope in a coolie's hand seems positively to have a soporific effect on him . . .

(205)

In E.M. Forster's *A Passage to India*, during the momentous trial of Dr Aziz, accused of molesting Adela Quested in the Marabar Caves, Adela who is in the witness box is drawn to the fine physique of the punka-wallah. Forster writes:

> The Court was crowded and of course very hot, and the first person Adela noticed in it was the humblest of all who were present, a person who had no bearing officially upon the trial: the man who pulled the punkah. Almost naked, and splendidly formed, he sat on a raised platform near the back, in the middle of the central gangway, and he caught her attention as she came in, and he seemed to control the proceedings . . . divine, yet he was of the city, its garbage had nourished him, [and] he would end on its rubbish heaps.
>
> (217)

In the midst of the traumatic trial where she has to declare that Aziz indeed did molest her, Forster's narrative alters the mood and tempo of the events. In the heavily racist atmosphere of the court, where an Indian is being, effectively, charged with an oversexed nature vis-à-vis the white woman, Forster represents the Englishwoman as intensely aware of the native man's body. This subtly complicates the stance taken by the British in the court. Maybe it was the not the native male who was fascinated by the white woman: Adela's attention to the punkah-wallah's body suggests quite the opposite.

Qazi

According to Muslim religious law, a qazi was a judge.

In British India qazis were appointed as advisers to the English judges in the *sadr diwani* courts, and in this they followed the Mughal system. From the 1770s the number of qazis and faujdars in criminal courts increased, although Warren Hastings sought to temper this influx by replacing the faujdars with English magistrates.

Muslim law officers were deemed to be important enough for the judicial system that Hastings set up the Calcutta Madrasa to ensure a steady supply of such qualified Muslim officers. Hastings also commissioned an English translation of the *Hidaya*, the Muslim law digest, for use in the courts.

In 1861 the appointment of qazis was also stopped. Muslim law therefore was no longer administered after the qazi-ul-khillat post was abolished. The National Muhammedan Association petitioned the government to revive the appointment of the qazis in 1872 because Muslim personal law was not being accounted for within the judicial system. With the compiling of Muslim law, starting with C. Hamilton, William MacNaghtan and others from the last decades of the eighteenth century, the British officials decided that they were competent enough to administer the law without taking recourse to Muslim advisers.

Qui hai/koi-hai

This term has been dated to the early nineteenth century in the Bengal Presidency, and refers primarily to a form of address, but also to a class of Englishmen in India. The Englishman walking into his bungalow would expect to be met by his entire retinue of personal attendants, to attend to the taking off of his shoes, jacket and to provide the nimbupani. It was also the call the English officer used when he entered the cantonment mess hall, seeking the attendants. 'the common call, Qui hi! (meaning 'who is there?') often rouses a dozen of the slumbering crew, though it is occasionally repeated, with some vociferation too, before one will stir', writes Thomas Williamson in his 1810 work, *East India Vade-Mecum*, or, Complete Guide to Gentlemen Intended for the Civil, Military, or Naval Service of the Hon. East India Company (1810).

'Qui hai' was the call issued by the Englishman, literally asking 'anyone there', although very often, the entire team would be ready and waiting, with notice of the sahib's arrival having been transmitted from the gates of the house itself. The very act of calling out when the servants were clearly visible was part of the imperial ethos that rendered the natives/servants invisible: so the sahib was literally asking if anybody was to be *seen*.

As Bernard Cohn (1996), David Cannadine (2002) and others have demonstrated, British power in India required spectacles, displays and rituals and the qui hais were one such exercise. The qui hai call was a theatrical strategy of the British in the colony. It ensured that the native servants were to understand that they were invisible in the power structure. As a constituent of imperial self-fashioning, the qui hais – essentially the Nabobs of Bengal – enacted a spectacle of power.

Every encounter of the British man with the native was to be an imperial display that also inserted the native into the display as an appendage or prop, part of what Cannadine terms 'a cavalcade of impotence' (121).

Rickshaw

The term is derived from the Japanese jin-rickshaw, meaning 'by human power'. It was sometimes referred to as jenny-rickshaw in British India. The rickshaw was a covered carriage for one person pulled along by one coolie and was very common in Calcutta from the nineteenth century. A rickshaw carrying a dead woman is the subject of Kipling's ghost story, 'The Phantom Rickshaw'.

Sahibs

In complete contrast to the nabob was the sahib. Carrying connotations in the local languages of 'master', the 'sahib' was at once an honorific and a class title. In local contexts, especially when describing royal families, the term signified a position in the hierarchy.

In the British Empire the sahib was a category of Englishman who belonged, usually, to the upper classes in English society back home. Very often the sahibs in India belonged to families with long histories of India service, such as the Metcalfes, the Cavendish-Bentincks, the Rivett-Carnacs and the Lawrences. The sahib was characterized as an upright Englishman out in India to keep the peace: fair but tough, wise and stoic. Made famous by figures like Cornwallis, William Jones, William Bentinck, Ellenborough and others in the nineteenth century, the sahib was the Englishman on the spot. He could be relied upon to make the correct decision without awaiting orders from the Board of Control. But more important than this ability to take the appropriate decision was the sahib's commitment to both the imperial task and India. The sahibs were at the forefront of the reform and civilizational missions in India – Bentinck's ban on *sati* in 1829 being only the first of many. Thus, while the nabob only saw India as a source of profit, the sahib saw the subcontinent as a field of activity, of self-sacrifice and duty. Many of them learnt numerous Indian languages (Jones knew 14), acquired a serious interest in Indian arts, literature and crafts and were often at the forefront of translation and conservation projects for Indian languages, literature and architecture.

Several of the sahibs were magistrates and soldiers. They were of course veterans of war – John Nicholson, the 'hero of Delhi', was one such, having made his fame/notoriety in Afghanistan when he was called to help reclaim Delhi during 1857. They also commanded, as a result of either bravery on the field of battle or reformist zeal or their commitment to justice, respect from the Indian subjects. As Ronny Heaslop would say in E.M. Forster's *A Passage to India* (1924), 'We're not out here for the purpose of behaving pleasantly ... We're out here to do justice and keep the peace' (49–50), thus capturing the sentiments of a sahib in India.

Sati/Suttee

For the European, the suttee represented the finest evidence of Indian, and particularly Hindu, barbarism. The British documented suttee for several decades, with travellers, statesmen, company officials, soldiers, missionaries all writing eye-witness or reported accounts of the ritual. The woman being led to the funeral pyre of her husband as a *sati* was the subject of William Skelton's engraving after William Hodges's account in *Travels in India, during the Years 1780, 1781, 1782, and 1783* (1793), and numerous descriptions through the entire colonial period. The accounts examined the ritual from legal, scriptural (Hindu, Christian), moral, humanitarian angles, agreed that it was barbaric. Fragile, mourning, divested of all the appurtenances of her marital life, treated as an evil omen by several people in her own families, the widow is the ultimate symbol of the vulnerable Asian woman in English colonial writings on India (Nair 1996).

It was not always easy to be an eye-witness to the *sati*. Claudius Buchanan wrote in 1819: 'unless an Englishman comes casually upon the scene, he never can, generally speaking, see a burning. The only expedient is, to desire your Hindoo servants to mention when they hear that one is about to take place' (iii–iv). William Ward the missionary claimed he was an eye-witness to many such instances (*An Account of the Writings, Religion and Manners of the Hindoos*), and elsewhere documented 250 *sati*s in Bengal alone (1822, 3: 308–41).

From the 1790s and early 1800s the Company officials, statesmen and missionaries sought to first solicit British public opinion against the Hindu practice – although it had been Company and government policy not to interfere in the religious beliefs and practices of the natives. This opinion-making took the form of detailed commentaries in the British press, evangelical reports and eye-witness accounts structured in order to suggest that the Indian women were crying out to the British public to save them from their own religious practices. For instance, James Peggs, a missionary, titled his work *India's Cries to British Humanity* (1830) and cited the oldest recorded mentions of the practice. He also cited the various petitions submitted to the British government by English civil society in England. Peggs called for the English nation as a whole to contribute to bringing about its end. Others were not certain that England ought to intervene, and a commentator in the *Missionary Register* of December 1823 was of the opinion that 'a law might doubtless be promulgated for the abolition of this practice without causing any serious disturbance' (564–5).

Eyewitness accounts were written in tones full of horror:

> It was impossible to hear the woman, had she groaned, or even cried aloud, on account of the mad noise of the people, and it was impossible for her to stir or struggle, on account of the bamboos, which are held down upon them like the levers of a press. We made much objection to their using these bamboos, and insisted it was using force to prevent the woman getting up, when the fire burnt her. But they declared it was only done to keep the pile from falling down. We could not bear to see more, but left them, exclaiming loudly against the murder, and full horror at what he had seen.
>
> (*The Weekly Entertainer*, 25 June 1804)

A review in *Gentleman's Magazine* of J.Z. Holwell's comments on *sati* notes: 'Mr H says he has been present at many of these sacrifices: in some, the victims, he observed a pitiable dread, tremor, and reluctance, that strongly spoke repentance for their declared resolution' (36 [1767]: 13). After a detailed account of a *sati* witnessed, Hartley Kennedy bursts into anguished rhetoric:

> These tombs [of the *sati* women] are painfully numerous in some sites, and apparently of the most remote antiquity. The heart bleeds to think of the scenes of human suffering and wretchedness they commemorate, – the bloodshed and the wrongs, – all man's violence and cruelty, and woman's faithfulness! Let us hope that a new day has dawned on India, and that these wretched sacrifices may be spoken of by future generations as things that were, before British dominion enlightened India . . .
>
> (*Bentley's Miscellany*, March 1843)

The government also sought to compile statistical and empirical accounts. Thus *sati* records were organized district-wise in Bengal and other places, arranged year-wise, as for example, in *Parliamentary Papers*, No. 443 (1824), *Parliamentary Papers*, No. 518 (1825) and elsewhere. Between 1815 and 1824, the British documented 6,632 cases in Bengal, Bombay, and Madras. Other commentators like Edward Thompson's in *Suttee: A Historical and Philosophical Inquiry* (1928), examined the clans, communities and castes where the practice was prevalent, and linked the practice to particular forms of worship. Thus, for instance, Thompson notes that *sati* was less prevalent among the Vaishnavas.

When the colonial government sought to enact laws, William Bentinck initiated an interesting process. He consulted religious scholars to seek clarity on the scriptural evidence for the practice. 'Having received from the Supreme Government a copy of the Regulation enacted by the Governor General in Council, for declaring the practice of Suttee to be illegal, we carefully examined all the texts of Hindoo Law which bear upon this subject. . . .' This was the letter from the Governor General in Council of Fort St George, Madras, to the Court of Directors, dated 12 February 1830 (*Parliamentary Papers*, No. 550, 1830).

Regulations governing *sati* quoted extensively from the *Manusmriti* and other texts, identifying Hindu scriptural and religious pronouncements on the practice. Thus W.H. Turnbull in *Parliamentary Papers* (No.749, 1821) issued orders to the effect that, if there has been a *sati*, the local police officer had to enquire and determine: 'if it appear that the widow had not attained her 16th year, or was not qualified to become a *suttee* under the provisions of the Shaster'. Peggs claimed that the practice 'has no foundation in any peculiar command given in the shastras' (26). Others criticized British laxity in banning the ritual, and Thomas Rowlandson the noted visual artist and caricaturist satirized the British attitude in a painting where he depicted Warren Hastings, the Governor General of British India, accepting a bribe to allow the *sati* to continue (the widow is on the pyre holding her husband's corpse, while Hastings is to one side of the picture, being bribed by the brahmins).

The debate therefore revolved around the religiously approved mode of *sati* in these texts. Another letter from the Governor General in Council of Bombay to the Court of Directors, dated 25 June 1823, in similar fashion, observes that in one case 'a widow burning with the bones of her deceased husband . . . is understood to be at variance with the Hindoo law' (*Parliamentary Papers*, No. 443, 1824). Arthur Steele's consultation with native pundits on the subject was documented in *Parliamentary Papers* (1788, 1830). The pundits were queried and their responses documented. For instance, as follows:

Question to the Pundits of the Nizamut Adawlut:

> *As it sometimes happens among persons professing the Hindoo religion, that upon the death of a man his widow becomes a suttee, i.e. burns herself with the body of her deceased husband, you are therefore asked, whether a woman is enjoined by the Shaster voluntarily to burn herself with the body of her husband, or is prohibited; and what are the conditions prescribed by the Shaster on such occasions? You are desired to give an answer in the course of fifteen days. 4th March 1805.*
>
> Answer. Having duly considered the question proposed by the court, I now answer it to the best of my knowledge:— Every woman, of the four castes (Brahmin, khetry, bues and soodur) is permitted to burn herself with the body of her husband, provided she has not infant children, nor is pregnant, nor in a state of uncleanness, nor under the age of puberty; in any of which cases she is not allowed to burn herself with her husband's body.
>
> But a woman who has infant children, and can procure another person to undertake the charge of bringing them up, is permitted to burn.
>
> It is contrary to law, as well as to the usage of the country, to cause any woman to burn herself against her wish, by administering drugs to stupefy or intoxicate her.
>
> When women burn themselves, they pronounce the sunkulp, and perform other prescribed ceremonies previously to burning.
>
> This rests upon the authority of Anjira, Vijasa and Vrihaspati mooni.
>
> (*Parliamentary Papers*, Vol. 18, No. 749, 1821)

William Bentinck's (1829) Minute on *sati* acknowledged that the prohibition might result in social upheavals among the Hindus but, he went on:

> I can conceive the possibility of the expression of dissatisfaction and anger being immediately manifested upon this

supposed attack on their religious usages, but the distant danger seems to me altogether groundless, provided that perfect respect continues to be paid to all their innocent rites and ceremonies, and provided also that a kind and considerate regard be continued to their worldly interests and comforts.

In 1829 through Regulation XVII of the Bengal Code, *sati* was outlawed:

> The practice of suttee, or of burning or burying alive the widows of Hindoos, is hereby declared illegal, and punishable by the Criminal Courts.

Studies of the *sati* abolition discourse have noted that women's lives and deaths became, for the British, a ready index for the decadent nature of Indian civilization in general and of Hindus in particular, but was substantially supported by the Indian middle class and intelligentsia in Bengal and other places. The Hindu woman was either dominated by the Hindu men, or she was victimized by religion, and the British discourse constructed a clear binary between voluntary and forced *sati* (Mani 1998). The colonial discourse around *sati*, as Lata Mani has shown, was interested in defining a cultural tradition. The condition of Indian women was a site where traditions could be examined and reformed by the colonial ruler.

British fiction and poetry utilized *sati* as a recurrent theme for the same purpose – of highlighting Hindu barbarity and British responsibility. The widow goes smilingly to her death in 'The Tomb of Suttee':

> E'en now one shudder as she mounts the pile:
> The struggle passes; with a calm delight
> She takes his head upon her breast – her smile
> Is hid by flames that, odorous and bright,
> Rise canopied with smoke.
> (Keene 1868: 133)

In G.H. Trevor's 'The Suttee of Gorah's Wife' (1894), the young widow, on seeing her husband's body on the pyre, and 'the spirit of the Rajput glowing/within her breast that swelled with love and pride' says 'my Lord will chide me for delay' and 'sprang on the pyre' (33). However, Rudyard Kipling's 'The Last Suttee' we see a reluctant *sati*: the queen unwilling to face the thought of death by burning has to be cut down by a sword instead.

The rescue of the *sati* became a key theme in British civilizational politics. An early instance of the *sati* discourse in literary representations occurs in Dryden's play *Aureng-zebe*. Aurangzeb believes *sati* as a sign of the wives' loyalty (V.1):

> 'Tis the procession of a funeral vow,
> Which cruel laws to Indian wives allow
> When fatally their virtue approve;
> Cheerful in flames, and martyrs of their love.
> (1808: 279)

Two *Muslim* women, Melesinda and Nourmahal, commit *sati*. Nourmahal's death is also cast in the form of a *sati* by Dryden:

> burn, I more than burn; I am all fire.
> See how my mouth and nostrils flame expire!
> I'll not come near myself
> Now I'm a burning lake, it rolls and flows;
> I'll rush, and pour it all upon my foes.
> Pull, pull that reverend piece of timber near:
> Throw't on, 'tis dry, 'twill burn
> Ha, ha! how my old husband crackles there!
> Keep him down, keep him down; turn him about:
> I know him, he'll but whiz, and strait go out.
> Fan me, you winds: What, not one breath of air?
> I'll burn them all, and yet have flames to spare.
> Quench me: Pour on whole rivers. Tis in vain:
> Morat stands there to drive them back again:
> With those huge billows in his hands, he blows
> New fire into my head: My brain-pan glows.
> See! see! there's Aureng-Zebe too takes his part;
> But he blows all his fire into my heart.
> (280)

In General Mainwaring's (1830) novel, *The Suttee*, the task of the English is to 'emancipate the Hindoos from the bondage of superstition' (cited in Herman 2005: 248). In Sydney Owenson's *The Missionary* (1811), Luxima is excommunicated from her Hindu identity *and* her Christian one. By committing *sati*, Luxima eventually demonstrates her primary loyalty to Hinduism (Gilmartin 1997).

Sati had its echoes in the women's campaign for rights and equality in Britain as well. One of the better-known examples of the *sati* as trope occurs in *Jane Eyre*. Jane compares herself to a *sati*:

> 'I considered it a very natural and necessary one: he had talked of his future wife dying with him. What did he mean by such a pagan idea? I had no intention of dying with him – he might depend on that.'
> 'Oh, all he longed, all he prayed for, was that I might live with him! Death was not for such as I.' 'Indeed it was sun-soaked India, and going on to eventually devise the sola-topi as a key component of the protection against the tropical sun: I had as good a right to die when my time came as he had: but I should bide that time, and not be hurried away in a suttee.'
> (233)

As late as the 1970s, discussing the failure of the Englishwoman, Paul Scott would describe Edwina Crane's suicide as a *sati*. In his *Raj Quartet*, Scott writes of her death:

> She dressed for the first time in her life in a white saree, the saree for her adopted country, the whiteness of widow-hood and mourning . . . She locked herself in and soaked the walls with paraffin and set them alight and died.
> (1978: 123)

Scott terms it 'suttee' (123).

Sepoy

This word is from the Hindi *sipahi*, meaning soldier. The term was used exclusively for Indian soldiers in the East India Company army.

The renewal of the Company's Charter in 1683 allowed them the right to raise armed fleets and armies to protect their various factories. In the 1688–90 period the Company waged war against Aurangzeb, and this war was instrumental in reinforcing the Company's insistence on military power in India.

From the early seventeenth century the three Presidencies raised and maintained their own armies, with salaries generated from the revenues in India itself. Europeans who had come out as soldiers, unfortunately, were often intemperate, quarrelsome and prone to tropical diseases. These were factors in the shift to native sepoys for, as T.A. Heathcote points out in his study, Indian soldiers were easier to maintain and discipline and were more or less immune to local diseases (29).

It was under Clive that a professionally trained army was put together. Stringer Lawrence was the first Commander-in-Chief. Clive was instrumental in putting together the Bengal European Regiment in 1756 and decreed red coats as the uniform for the regiments. The officers of these regiments were always European. By 1760 the Indian sepoys were integral to the Company's armed forces.

The sepoys were initially drawn from the Bihar region (and so were called *purabiyas/poorbeahs*, or easterners), many of whom came from communities and families who had served the Mughal armies. They were recruited through an intermediary and through known contacts.

With the martial races theory gaining strength in the late eighteenth and early nineteenth centuries, the sepoys were drawn from specific communities like the Sikhs, who were seen as the 'warrior castes'. The army was one of the largest employers for Indians in the days of Empire. As Nile Green points out, the 'Indian Army was no less a source of employment, pride and identity for the millions of Indians and their dependents' (2). They received decent pay, uniforms and an identity as a soldier.

After the Company was disbanded in 1858, the native regiments continued to exist until 1895 when all Presidency armies were abolished, to make way for the Indian army.

Shikari

The term derives from the Hindi *shikar*, meaning hunt and *shikari*, meaning a hunter. In the colony, the term, as applied to the Englishman, and occasionally the woman, signified several things.

The shikari was, above all else, portrayed as the truly masculine Englishman, seeking adventure and risk in the colony. The hunt served as a means of demonstrating masculinity, English grit and resourcefulness and even a particular tradition of hunting that was, supposedly, truly English in spirit (MacKenzie 1987, 1988, Mangan 1992, Pandian 2001, McDevitt 2004, Pablo Mukherjee 2005). Sporting memoirs, especially in the 1880–1930 period, document dramatic encounters with tigers, wild boar, crocodiles and assorted jungle creatures.

> To meet face to face a surly boar, having tusks that would badly 'rip' an elephant, and who resents your intrusive approach – to

note the stealthy, slouching gait of some lithe leopard, stalking the peaceful antelope or graceful spotted deer . . . or howling wolves, is a revelation of savage animal life that one does not soon forget.

(Inglis 1892: 2–3)

Later Inglis would describe the actual encounter:

And, most thrilling of all, to see the convulsive upward leap, and hear the throttled gasping roar of a wounded tiger, as the whiff of powder smoke from your trusty gun salutes you like grateful incense – that's one of the sensations that makes the dull pulses throb and quicken their beat.

(3)

The voluntary questing for risk and danger, and the subsequent conquest of the same, generated an extreme exotic (Nayar 2008) of the colony when all of the colonial territory had been mapped and domesticated. As a test of Englishness, then, the shikari had to venture forth into hitherto uncharted areas.

The shikari was also the saviour of villagers and rural folk from predators. Henry Shakespeare writes:

To him who has been blessed with the gifts of good nerve, energy and strength, that he may save the bodies of these same ignorant heathen from the fell destroyer that lives in the forest and preys upon them. Who shall say that the poor idolater saved by the latter from destruction shall not become converted to Christianity by the former?

(1862: 3)

Numerous shikari memoirs from the period offer this rescue trope, so that the Englishman's pleasure in the hunt is rendered secondary to his ardent desire to rid the poor Indian folk of their troubling predator.

The shikari of course hunted with the aid of large retinues of native beaters and assistants, all made available, more often, by the local rajahs. The social apparatus of the white man's hunt, then, was itself a mode of enforcing colonial social relations where the natives were suppliers of the materials and apparatuses of hunting, and the white man would eventually iconize himself and be iconized as the true hero with no reference to the native helpers.

The shikari, in other words, was a version of the colonial conquistador, placing his life at risk in order to tame the brutal landscape and its fauna.

Sicca

It originally meant a newly minted rupee coin, to distinguish it from a worn or old coin. The sicca was valued higher than the older coin. In 1793 the British government in Bengal decided to do away with this distinction. A regulation was passed that set the coin minted in the 19th year of Shah Alam, the Mughal emperor, as the legal tender, and this was designated the *19 san sikkah*. However, another key distinction remained. The sicca had 192 grains troy and 176. 13 grains of silver, which was greater than what the East India Company's rupee (introduced in 1835, and was a version of the Farruckabad rupee, although the Company was authorized by the British Crown to mint coins as far back as 1677) contained.

This discrepancy was noted, and its implications for computing the trade and profits of the Company studied:

> Now the consequence of this over valuation of the current rupee that is the difference 1s 9.177 d and 2s has been the giving a false view not only of the statement account between England and India but also a statement equally false of the profit and on goods exported to India and of goods imported from India . . .
>
> From this it is apparent that by departing from the real par value of the Indian and currencies in the accounts and statements and an arbitrary or imaginary value all the Company's exports as well as their imports have suffered a corresponding diminution in all the statements furnished from time to time The evil of this procedure has been twofold for first the exports have been charged less for prime cost in Indian books than they should have been charged which has shown a profit where there none and second the imports have been charged more for prime cost in the home than they should have been charged which has shown a loss where there might been a profit.
>
> To obviate this in future it is submitted that instead of continuing the present arbitrary valuation of the Indian monies the real par value should be taken in all the future which is

KEYWORDS

as follows Sicca rupee 2s o 566d Arcot rupee 1 s 11.247 d 1 s 11.004 d.
(Extract from the Report of the Committee of Accounts, dated 13 April 1814, *Report from the Select Committee on the Affairs of the East India Company – II Finance and Accounts-Trade*, 1832: 295)

Regulation VII of 1833 altered the weight of the Calcutta and Farruckabad rupees: Calcutta sicca rupee would weigh 192 grains, and the Farruckabad rupee would weigh 180 grains (*Sessional Papers* [House of Lords] *1837–38*, Vol. VIII, 1838: 19).

The sicca survived as tender well into the nineteenth century until it was abolished in 1836, although Alexander del Mar's *A History of Monetary Systems* dates the 'demonetization and withdrawal of sicca rupees' to 1838 (1901: 397).

Sircar/circar
It meant simply 'government'.

Sola-topi
The British were deeply concerned about the effects of the tropical sun on their constitutions. Extensive medical documentation and prescriptions to prevent 'sunstroke' or 'heat apoplexy', described as 'injury' appeared from the last decades of the eighteenth century (Harrison 1994).

The credit of inventing the sola-topi, according to anthropologist Bernard S. Cohn, goes to Julius Jefferies, a doctor serving in India. Cohn reports on Jefferies's extensive writing on the link between clothing and disease in sun-soaked India, and eventually devised the sola-topi as a key component of the protection against the tropical sun (Cohn 1996: 153).

The sola-topi was made of vegetable fibre from the pith of the sola plant. While effective against the Indian sun, it would collapse when wet, and so was useless once monsoon set in. It also had in some models khaki cloth overhanging at the front and back to keep the sun away from eyes and neck. There was a variant of the sola-topi made of cork which was more durable in sun and rain, and some sahibs got it enamelled to waterproof it.

The sola-topi was usually worn with a turban wrapped around it. It was part of the day-wear for the British in India, and it was deemed to be inappropriate to wear it after sunset. The sola-topi was also ungendered as costume, being worn by men, women and children alike.

The sola-topi was worn only by the British, and this item of their dress code was also, therefore, a marker of their distinction from their colonized subjects (Cohn). Eurasians also took to wearing sola-topis to indicate their affiliation – by blood – to the ruling races.

Subedar/subahdar

A man in charge of a suba, which was a district in the Mughal Empire, was called a subedar and was equivalent of a governor and the head of the administration therein.

Under the East India Company (EIC), the subedar was a native officer in charge of a company of sepoys, and was the highest native officer in the regiment. The subedar would report to a European sergeant. In Sita Ram's *From Sepoy to Subedar* (1873), he writes:

> I was promoted to *Subedar* after forty-eight years of hard wear and tear in the *Sirkar's* service. I entered the army under the flag of the Company *Bahadur*, and I ended under the flag of the Empress of the World. I was an old man of sixty five years of age and had attained the highest rank to be gained in the Native Army, but I would have been much better fitted for this position thirty years earlier. What could I do now at the head of my Company? How could I double-march, or perform Light Infantry drill? But I was expected to be as active as ever and no allowance was made for my forty-eight years' service. No one bothered to remember that I had carried a musket for thirty years and 'had been present in as many battles as most of the officers had lived years. I was shouted at by the Adjutant as if I was a bullock, and he a mere boy, young enough to be my grandson. I was abused by the Commanding Officer, and called a fool, a donkey, and an old woman! Finally I was taken before the Commander-in-Chief and reported on as being utterly useless – a man the Commanding Officer could do nothing with . . . The time it took to become a *Subedar* was far too long for most *sepoys* to aspire to, for this promotion was seldom given until after forty years' service. In recent years some men have become *Jemadars* and *Subedars* more quickly, and many of them were immediately promoted if they brought young men for enlistment during the Mutiny. This is a much better system . . .
>
> (172)

Sita Ram's tone captures much of the agony of native soldiers in the EIC army, with their delayed promotions and thwarted aspirations. The subedar position was clearly one much sought after, and Sita Ram notes that when it finally comes to him he is no longer a useful soldier but a pensioner.

Syce

Derived from the Arab *sais*, meaning 'groom', the syce was the horse-keeper in British India. They were called by different names in various Presidencies: 'ghorawalla' in Bombay, 'horsekeeper' in Madras (Steel and Gardiner 55). They were paid Rs 8 in Bengal, Rs 15 in Bombay and Rs 10 in Madras (Steel and Gardiner 55). The syce's wife also served as the grass-cutter (Steel and Gardiner 32).

The syce's duties were described thus in Steel and Gardiner's *The Complete Indian Housekeeper and Cook:*

> one syce to every three horses would, as a rule, be found sufficient. The syce should be made responsible for the horses under him, and any complaints he may make about the grass-cutters should be attended to at once. He is thus placed in a position of responsibility, and for the extra work involved may be given a small increase of wage. His duties also become those of an English groom. Every morning after breakfast he will come for orders, and again after dinner at night; since, if a horse is to be taken out early in the morning, a good syce will wish to know it, in order that he may arrange that the animal gets its food in good time. Without grasscutters two syces should be enough for three horses.
>
> (89)

And:

> The syce, however, has other duties besides keeping his horses. He must look after the saddlery and harness, also the dog-cart or carriage, unless a coachman is kept.
>
> (94)

The syce might accompany the sahib on his morning trot, carrying a whisk to keep off the flies that are 'very troublesome both to the horses and to their riders' (Williamson 1810: 129).

Thug/thugi

One of the most enduring colonial terms, and stereotypes, the thug was devil-worshipper, con-man, ruthless killer, drug-addicted robber, and, most of all, a hereditary killer–robber. The term took on several of these connotations through the nineteenth century and enabled the British government to dedicate money, men and resources to curb the practice. Novels and commentaries were produced about the practice and officials like W.H. Sleeman showcased themselves as heroes in their accounts of campaigns against the thugs. A vast amount of documentation, then, is available in the colonial archive on thugi. They were, in turn, deemed to be hereditary murderers, zealous members of a religious cult, or criminals belonging to a mysterious society.

In 1816 R. Sherwood published an essay, reprinted in the *Asiatic Researches*, titled 'Of the Murderers called Phansigars'. Sherwood linked robbery with Hinduism, attributing the actions of the robbers to the innate cruelty of their religion. Sherwood defined them as 'belong[ing] to a distinct class of hereditary murderers' (*Asiatic Researches* 13: 251). This association of robbery with devil-worship, Satanism and Hindu evil is reinforced through the nineteenth century. J.A.R. Stevenson's piece, 'Some Account of the Phansigars, or Gang-Robbers and of the Shudgarshids, or Tribes of Jugglers' in the *Journal of the Royal Asiatic Society* described them as a 'race of vampires undeserving of the name of man' (1834: 283). W.H. Sleeman claimed that 'the murders they perpetrate are pleasing to her . . . The Deity according to their belief, guides and protects them' (1836: i). Meadows Taylor in his *Confessions of a Thug* (1839) presents the thug swearing by the goddess Bhawani and the Koran.

Thugi was also associated with Indian, specifically Hindu, antiquity. This line of argument enabled the British government to show Hinduism itself as depraved from its very ancient days and social, law-and-order problems such as thugi being as old as Indian civilization. In other words, thugi in colonial thought was a sign of India's pre-modern, barbaric and uncivilized past.

Another interpretation of the practice of the 'stranglers' – because thugs garrotted their victims with handkerchiefs and scarves – was that they constituted a secret society. Sleeman in his 'The Secret Societies of Asia – the Assassins and Thugs' in *Blackwood's Edinburgh* (49 [1841]: 229) argued this case, for instance. Similar views were expressed in Meadows Taylor's *Confessions of a Thug*, John Shakespeare's (1820) essay 'Regarding Badheks and T'hegs' in *Asiatic*

Researches 13, Edward Thornton's (1837) work, *Illustrations of the History and Practices of Thugs*.

The result of the classification of some castes and communities as hereditary killer–robbers was the Criminal Tribes and Castes Act, which enabled the British government to designate numerous vagrant and often impoverished castes and communities such as the Pindaris as criminal by *birth*. The Act read:

> Whoever shall be proved to have belonged, either before or after the passing of this Act, to any gang of Thugs, either within or without the Territories of the East India Company, shall be punished with imprisonment for life, with hard labour.
> (cited in Field 1870: 62)

Such communities were placed under surveillance and were often subject to repeated police searches, arrests and beatings. A massive antithugi campaign was underway by the 1830s. Sleeman in *Report on the Depredations Committed by the Thug Gangs of Upper and Central India* (1840) proposed the preparation of a database of thugs. Thugi was deemed to be a defiance of the colonial regime that demanded swift punitive action (Arnold 1986).

Fiction produced about thugs included celebrated texts like Meadows Taylor's *Confessions of a Thug* (1839). As late as 1952 John Masters published his novel on the same theme, *The Deceivers*. Other texts, such as Fanny Parkes's travelogue *Wanderings of a Pilgrim in Search of the Picturesque*, also claims that thugs confessed to being devotees of the goddess Bhawani (1850, 1: 129).

Contemporary commentators have noted the many layers in the representations of thugi, from typical Orientalist biases and preconceptions (Van Woerkens 2002) to Evangelical Protestant ethics (Wagner 2004) and the transformation of the practice into a pan-Indian phenomenon so as to present it as part of the subcontinent's 'national character' (Macfie 2008). The discourse of secrecy enabled the government to step up surveillance (Parama Roy 1998). The thugi discourse transformed India into a land of enormous danger with religious cults of robber–murderers sweeping across the land – an image that quickly captured British public imagination (Singha 2000).

Tiffin

Tiffin was either a light lunch or a snack, not necessarily consumed at meal times. It may have been derived from 'tiffing', to eat or drink between meals, and related to 'tiff' meaning to imbibe a small quantity of alcoholic stimulants.

Sundays would mean curry tiffin in places like Singapore and Malaysia, an elaborate and relaxed lunch, effectively. But even in India the Sunday tiffin was a massive meal. Flora Annie Steel and Grace Gardiner write:

> Heavy luncheons or tiffins have much to answer for in India. It is a fact scarcely denied, that people at home invariably eat more on Sundays, because they have nothing else to do; so in the hot weather out here people seem to eat simply because it passes the time. It is no unusual thing to see a meal of four or five distinct courses placed on the table, when one light entree, and a dressed vegetable would be ample. Even when guests are invited to tiffin, there is no reason why they should be tempted to over-eat themselves, as they too often are, by the ludicrously heavy style of the ordinary luncheon party in India. If the object of such parties is, as it should be, to have a really pleasant time for sociable conversation between lunch and afternoon tea, stuffing the guests into a semi-torpid state certainly does not conduce to success. Yet if the menu be large and long, it is almost impossible for a luncheon guest to persist in refusal without making himself remarkable.
>
> (47)

Williamson in *East India Vade-Mecum* wrote:

> a little avant diner commonly called a tiffing and known among us by the name of lunch. This kind of refreshment (for it is not considered a repast) usually takes place between one and two o'clock, and consists of grilled fowls, mutton chops, cold meats, and sometimes of curry and rice.
>
> (1810, 2: 111)

In the late 1890s 'tiffin lunches' would be served in The Raffles Hotel in London.

Eventually, tiffin simply came to describe the lunchbox.

Writer
The writer was originally the copying clerk in the East India Company (EIC)'s factories. They were also recording and documentation

officers, writing up reports, decisions and Minutes accounts and shipping logs. They were hired from the natives but Europeans were also appointed to the job.

Instructions for those Englishmen seeking employment as writers included in John Gilchrist's *The General East India Guide and Vade Mecum* (1825), besides specificities of costume (such as military gloves and crimson silk sash):

> Gilchrist's English and Hindoostanee Dictionary; British Indian Monitor, Guide and Storyteller; Dialogues; Persian Rudiments, Hindoostanee and Persian Vocabulary.

(535)

The firm Welch and Stalker advertised 'Necessaries for a Writer to India' (reprinted in *Regulations as to the Nomination of Students at the East India College*, 1809: unpaginated).

Writing offices were earmarked within the factories. This segregation was intended to 'secure the integrity of the written documents through a combination of openness and closure' (Ogborn 101). Each writer was allotted a desk and had to perform all his duties in that room. Later this laborious task of copying would be entrusted to a public press.

In Calcutta, the writers were housed in a separate building, called the Writers' Building, built in 1777. The Writers' Building still stands, having served as the Secretariat of the West Bengal government for several years.

Later examinations were introduced for aspirants to writerships – the writers were now administrators as well – and had to attend college at the East India College, Haileybury, established in 1806. There were extensive debates in the English Parliament as to the desirability of such examinations as a form of recruitment of writers. Previously, these positions were filled by patronage, and a Select Committee of the House of Commons found that the entire process was rife with corruption in 1809. At a General Court of the EIC held at East India House in July 1809, it was ruled that 'in future all Writers and Cadets, as well as students meant for those appointments, shall be chosen in an open Court of Directors . . . by the interrogation of the candidate and the person recommending him' (*Regulations as to the Nomination of Students at the East India College*, 1809: unpaginated). Passing four terms at Haileybury was deemed to qualify a person to be a writer, by an Act renewed in 1826.

Charles Lamb, the essayist, joined the EIC as a writer, and was paid a sum of £40 annually as salary according to the data for 1795. J.S. Mill joined the EIC as a clerk in 1823 and went on to become the Examiner of Indian Correspondence. Contemporary genealogy projects have been involved in compiling data for the identities of people employed as labourers and writers in the EIC's London offices (British Library, London's 'Untold Lives' Project).

BIBLIOGRAPHY

Primary sources

A Handbook for Travellers in India, Burma, and Ceylon. London: John Murray and Calcutta: Thacker, Spink, & Co., 1911.

A Lady Resident. *The Englishwoman in India*. London: Smith, Elder, & Co., 1864.

Annual Report on the Lock Hospitals of the Madras Presidency, for the Year 1877. Madras: R. Hill, at the Government Printing Press, 1878. http://digital.nls.uk/75112080. Accessed 25 January 2016.

Anon. 'The Manufacture of Fine Muslins at Dacca', *Alexander's East India and Colonial Magazine* 9 (1835): 432–34.

———. *The Case of Fann-Makers, Who Have Petitioned the Honourable House of Commons against the Importation of Fans from the East-Indies*. Broadside: np, 1670.

The Asiatic Journal and Monthly Register for British India and Its Dependencies 22 (1837): 317–24.

Atkinson, George F. *Curry and Rice of Forty Plates; or, the Ingredients of Social Life at 'Our Station' in India*. 1859. London: Day and Son, nd. 3rd ed.

Austen, Jane. *Mansfield Park*. 1814. Ed. John Lucas. London: Oxford University Press, 1970.

Baden-Powell, R. S. S. *Pig-Sticking or Hoghunting: A Complete Account for Sportsmen and Others*. London: Harrison and Son, 1889.

Bellew, F. J. [Captain]. *Memoirs of a Griffin, or, a Cadet's First Year in India*. London: W. H. Allen, 1880.

Bernier, François. *Travels in the Mogul Empire*. London: W. Pickering, 1826. Vol. II.

Beveridge, Henry. *A Comprehensive History of India, Civil, Military and Social*. London: Blackie and Sons, 1862.

Bolts, William. *A Consideration on Indian Affairs*. London: J. Almon, 1772.

Boulger, Demetrius C. *Lord William Bentinck*. Oxford: Clarendon Press, 1897.

Bowrey, Thomas. *A Geographical Account of Countries Round the Bay of Bengal 1669 to 1679*. 1905. Ed. R. C. Temple. New Delhi: Munshiram Manoharlal, 1997.

Briggs, John. 'Account of the Origin, History, and Manners of the Race of Men called Bunjaras', *Transactions of the Literary Society of Bombay* 1 (1819): 170–97.

Brodie, D. *A Little Book of Little Manners for Young Indians: A Concise Manual of for Young Indians*, 1912.

Brontë, Charlotte. *Jane Eyre*. 1847. Ed. Richard Dunn. New York: W. W. Norton, 2010.

———. *Villette*. 1853. Ed. Herbert Rosengarten and Margaret Smith. Oxford: Clarendon, 1984.

Bruton, William. *News from the East-Indies, or, a Voyage to Bengalla*. London: J. Oakes, 1638.

Buchanan, Claudius. *An Apology for Promoting Christianity in India*. London: T. Cadell and W. Davies, 1814.

———. 'Juggernaut in Bengal', in *The Works of Claudius Buchanan*. Ed. Buchanan. Baltimore: Neal and Wills, 1812. 27–28.

———. *Memoirs of the Life and Writings of the Rev. Claudius Buchanan*. By Hugh Pearson. London: Benjamin and Thomas Kite, 1817.

Buck, Edward J. *Simla, Past and Present*. Calcutta: Thacker, Spink & Co., 1904.

Burford, Robert. *Description of a View of the Island and Harbour of Bombay, Now Exhibiting at the Panorama, Leicester Square*. London: T. Brettell, 1831.

Burton, Richard. *Pilgrimage to Al-Medinah and Meccah*. New York: Dover Books, 1964.

Busteed, H. E. *Echoes from Old Calcutta*. 1888. New Delhi: Asian Educational Services, 1999.

Campbell, Joseph. *Baksheesh and Brahman: Asian Journals – India*. Ed. Robin and Stephen Larsen and Antony Van Couvering. 1956. Novato: New World Library, 2002.

Carey, W. H. *The Good Old Days of Honourable John Company*. Calcutta: R. Cambray, 1906. Vol. 1.

Chambers, William. *A Dissertation on Oriental Gardening*. London: W. Griffin, 1772.

Colebrooke, Henry. 'On the Sanscrit and Pracrit Languages', *Asiatic Researches* 7 (1803): 199–231.

'Commercial Intercourse with India', *Asiatic Journal and Monthly Register for British and Foreign India, China and Australasia*, New Series, 37.145 (1842): 1–17.

Cormack, John. *Account of the Abolition of Female Infanticide in Guzerat*. London: Black, Parry and Co., 1815.

Correspondence Exhibiting the Nature and Use of the Poona Duftur, and the Measures Adopted for Its Preservation and Arrangement since the Introduction of British Rule: A Selection of Papers Explanatory of the Origin of the Inam Commission: Selections from the Records of the Bombay Government, No. XXX, New Series. Bombay: Bombay Education Society, 1856.

Cotton, J. S. *Mountstuart Elphinstone*. Oxford: Clarendon, 1892.

BIBLIOGRAPHY

Cox, Edward. *The Regimental Moonshi*. London: W. H. Allen, 1847.

Croker, B. M. *To Let*. Philadelphia: JB Lippincott, 1906.

Crooke, William. *An Introduction to the Popular Religion and Folk-lore of Northern India*. 1894. New Delhi: Asian Educational Services, 1994.

Dale, T. F. *Polo: Past and Present*. London: Country Life, 1904.

Del Mar, Alexander. *A History of Monetary Systems*. 1895. New York: The Cambridge Encyclopedia Company, 1901.

Desai, Dinkar D. *Maritime Labour in India*. Bombay: Servants Society of India, 1940.

Diver, Maud. *Candles in the Wind*. London: John Lane, 1909.

———. *Lilamani: A Study in Possibilities*. London: Hutchinson, 1911.

Doyley, Charles. *The European in India*. 1813. New Delhi: Asian Educational Services, 1995.

Dryden, John. 'Aureng-Zebe, A Tragedy', in *The Works of John Dryden*. Ed. Walter Scott. London: William Miller, 1808. Vol. 5. 167–284.

Duncan, Sara Jeanette. *The Story of Sonny Sahib*. London: Macmillan, 1894.

Edgeworth, M. *The Grateful Negro*. 1804. The University of Adelaide Library. http://ebooks.adelaide.edu.au/e/edgeworth/maria/grateful-negro/. Accessed 18 July 2014.

El Edroos, Syed Fakhruddin Aboobaker. *Modern Indian Etiquette: Of Mixed Society, Describing Ancient Social Usages and Customs, Aiming at Social Amity Between Indians and Non-Indians*. Surat: H.R. Scott at the Mission Press, 1922.

Fanthome, J. F. *Mariam*. Benares: Chandraprabha Press, 1896.

Farwell, Christopher. *An East-India Colation*. London: Printed by B. A. and T. F., 1633.

Fay, Eliza. *The Original Letters from India*. Ed. Walter Kelly Firminger. Calcutta: Thacker, Spink & Co., 1909.

Fergusson, James. *Picturesque Illustration of Ancient Architecture in Hindustan*. London: J. Hogarth, George Barclay, 1848.

Field, C. D. *Chronological Table of and Index to the Indian Statute Book from the Year 1834*. London: Butterworths, 1870.

Forbes, Duncan. *Hindustani Manual*. 1845. Ed. Shamsul Ulama and M. Yusuf Jafri. London: Crosby Lockwood and Son, 1918. 22nd ed.

Forbes, James. *Oriental Memoirs: A Narrative of Seventeen Years Residence in India*. London: Richard Bentley, 1834. Vol I.

Forster, E. M. *A Passage to India*. Orlando, FL: Harcourt Brace Jovanovich, 1984.

Forster, George. *A Journey from Bengal to England through the Northern Part of India, Kashmire, Afghanistan and Persia, and into Russia, by the Caspian Sea*. London: R. Faulder, 1798. 2 vols.

Fort William-India House Correspondence XIII. Ed. P. G. Gupta. New Delhi: National Archives, 1959.

Foster, William (ed). *Letters Received by the East India Company from Its Servants in the East*. 1615. Vol. 3. London: Sampson Low, Marston & Company, 1899.

From *The Miracle of Purun Bhagat*, notes edited by Alan Underwood and John Radcliffe. Online at http://www.kiplingsociety.co.uk/rg_purun1.htm.

From *The Tamil Nadu Devadasis (Prevention of Dedication) Act, 1947*, by Tamil Nadu. Online at http://www.lawsofindia.org/statelaw/5285/TheTamilNadu DevadasisPreventionofDedicationAct1947.html.

From *CyberCoolies: Call center workers are the new slave laborers of the 21st century*, by Harish Trivedi. Online at http://www.littleindia.com/life/1507-cybercoolies.html.

From *Life's Handicap*, by Rudyard Kipling. Online at http://www.telelib.com/authors/K/KiplingRudyard/prose/LifesHandicap/headofdistrict.html

From *My Own True Ghost Story* by Rudyard Kipling, notes edited by John McGivering. Online at http://www.kiplingsociety.co.uk/rg_owntrue1.htm.

Fryer, John. *A New Account of East-India and Persia*. London: R. I. Chiswell, 1698.

Gilchrist, John Borthwick. *A Grammar of the Hindoostanee Language*. Calcutta: Chronicle Press, 1796.

———. *The General East India Guide and Vade Mecum*. London: Kingsbury, Parbury and Allen, 1825.

Goonam, Dr. *Coolie Doctor: An Autobiography*. 1991. Hyderabad: Orient BlackSwan, 1998.

Grainger, J. *Sugar-Cane: A Poem*. 1764. Early Americas Digital Archive. http://mith.umd.edu/eada/html/display.php?docs=grainger_sugarcane.xml. Accessed 20 July 2014.

Grant, James. *First Love Last Love: A Tale of the Indian Mutiny*. London: George Routledge and Sons, 1868. 3 vols.

Hadley, George. *Grammatical Remarks on the Practical and Vulgar Dialect of the Indostan Language, Commonly called Moors*. London: T. Cadell, 1772.

Halhed, Nathaniel B. *A Code of Gentoo Laws, or, the Ordinations of the Pundits*. London: np, 1776.

Heber, Reginald. *Narrative of a Journey Through the Upper Provinces of India, from Calcutta to Bombay, 1824–1825*. London: Carey, Lea and Carey, 1829. Vol. II.

Herbert, Thomas. *A Relation of Some Years Travel, Begun Anno 1626*. London: William Stansby and Jacob Bloome, 1634.

Hervey, H. J. A. *The Europeans in India*. London: S. Paul, 1913.

Hervey, H. *The European in India*. London: Stanley Paul, 1913.

Hodges, William. *Travels in India, during the Years 1780, 1781, 1782, and 1783*. 1793. New Delhi: Munshiram Manoharlal, 1999.

Home, W. E. *Merchant Seamen: Their Diseases and Their Welfare Needs*. London: John Murray, 1922.

Hood, W. H. *The Blight of Insubordination: The Lascar Question and the Rights and Wrongs of the British Shipmaster*. London: Spottiswoode, 1903.

Hutton, James. *A Popular Account of the Thugs and Dacoits, the Hereditary Garroters and Gang-Robbers of India*. London: Hutton, 1857.

BIBLIOGRAPHY

Inglis, James. *Tent Life in Tigerland*. London: Sampson Low, Marston & Company, 1892.

Kaye, John. *History of the Sepoy War in India*. 1864. London: W. H. Allen, 1875. 3 vols.

Kaye, John W. and G. B. Malleson. *History of the Indian Mutiny of 1857–58*. 1864. London: WH Allen, 1888. Vol. I.

Kaye, M. M. *Sun in the Morning*. London: Penguin, 1992.

Keene, H. G. 'The Tomb of the Suttee', in *Under the Rose: Poems Written Chiefly in India*. London: Bell and Daldy, 1868. 131–3.

Kindersley, Jemima. *Letters from the Island of Teneriffe, Brazil, the Cape of Good Hope, and the East Indies*. London: J. Nource, 1777.

Laffaye, Horace A. *The Evolution of Polo*. Jefferson: McFarland, 2009.

Lethbridge, Roper. *A Genealogical and Biographical Dictionary of the Ruling Princes, Chiefs, Nobles, and other Personages, Titled or Decorated of the Indian Empire*. London: Macmillan, 1893.

Letters Received by the East India Company from Its Servants in the East. 1615. Vol. 3. Ed. William Foster. London: Sampson Low, Marston & Company, 1899.

Locke, J. C. *The First Englishmen in India*. 1930. Delhi: Munshiram Manoharlal, 1997.

'The Machinery Used in Patna and Thiroot', *Alexander's East India and Colonial Magazine* 10 (1835): 148–57.

Majendie, Vivian Dering. *Up among the Pandies, or, a Year's Service in India*. London: Routledge, Warne, and Routledge, 1859.

Malcolm, John. 'Notes of Instructions to Assistants and Officers Acting under the Orders of Major-General Sir John Malcolm, GCB', in *A Memoir of Central India*. Ed. John Malcolm. London: Kingsbury, Parbury and Allen, 1823. Vol. 2. 433–75.

Masters, John. *Bhowani Junction*. London: Michael Joseph, 1954.

———. *Bhowani Junction*. London: Sphere, 1983.

Medwin, Thomas. 'The Pindarees', in *Sketches in Hindoostan and Other Poems*. Ed. Thomas Medwin. London: J. and C. Ollier, 1821.

Minutes of Evidence Taken before the Committee of the Whole House, and the Select Committee, on the Affairs of the East India Company. London: E. Cox and Sons, 1813.

Mitra, Deenbandhu. *Nildarpan, or the Indigo Planting Mirror*. Trans. Michael Madhusudan Dutt. Calcutta: C. H. Manuel, 1861.

Mundy, Peter. *The Travels of Peter Mundy in Europe and Asia, 1608–1667*. Cambridge: Hakluyt Society, 1907.

Nundy, A. 'The Eurasian Problem in India', *The Imperial and Asiatic Quarterly Review and Oriental and Colonial Record* 9.17–18 (1900): 56–73.

Orme, Robert. *A History of the Military Transactions of the British Nation in Indostan*. London: F. Wingrave, 1799.

Orme, Robert. *Historical Fragments of the Mogul Empire*. 1782. Ed. J. P. Guha. New Delhi: Associated, 1974.

BIBLIOGRAPHY

Ovington, John. *A Voyage To Suratt In The Year 1689.* London: Jacob Tonson, 1690.

———. *An Essay Upon the Nature and Qualities of Tea.* London: R. Roberts, 1699.

———. *A Voyage to Suratt in the Year 1689.* London: Jacob Tonson, 1696.

Owenson, Sydney. *The Missionary: An Indian Tale.* London: J. J. Reynolds, 1811. 3 vols.

Parkes, Fanny. *Wanderings of a Pilgrim in Search of the Picturesque.* London: P. Richardson, 1850.

Peggs, James. *India's Cries to British Humanity.* London: Seely, 1830.

Perrin, Alice. *The Woman in the Bazaar.* 1914. London: Cassell and Co., 1926.

Phillott, D. C. *Hindustani Manual.* Calcutta: np, 1913. 2nd ed.

Postans, J. 'Memorandum on the City of Shikarpoor, in Upper Sindh', *Journal of the Asiatic Society of Bengal*, New Series, 10 (1841): 17–26.

Prinsep, Augustus. *The Baboo.* London: Smith, Elder, 1834.

Prohibitions and Negations which mainly Govern Propriety in Every-Day Life. Calcutta: Dasgupta & Co., 1912.

Ram, Sita. *From Sepoy to Subedar: Being the Life and Adventures of Subedar Sita Ram, a Native Officer of the Bengal Army Written and Related by Himself.* 1873. Trans. James Thomas Norgate. Ed. James Lunt. New Delhi: Vikas, 1970.

Regulations as to the Nomination of Students at the East India College. London: Cox and Sons, 1809.

Report from the Select Committee on the Affairs of the East India Company – II: Finance and Accounts-Trade. London: House of Commons, 1832.

Roberts, Fred. *Letters Written during the Indian Mutiny.* 1924. New Delhi: Lal, 1979.

Roebuck, Thomas. *The Annals of the College of Fort William.* Calcutta: Philip Pereira, 1819.

Royal Commission on Opium. *Minutes of Evidence Taken before the Royal Commission on Opium, 1894.* London: Her Majesty's Stationery Office, 1894. Vol. 4.

———. *Final Report of the Royal Commission on Opium: Part 1. The Report.* London: Her Majesty's Stationery Office, 1895. Vol. 6.

Russell, R. V. *The Tribes and Castes of the Central Provinces.* London: Macmillan, 1916. Vol. 3.

Russell, W. H. *My Diary of India in the Year 1858–59.* London: Routledge, Warne and Routledge, 1860. 2 vols.

Savarkar, V. D. The Indian War of Independence, 1857. 1909. New Delhi: Asian Educational Services, 2014.

Scott, Paul. *The Jewel in the Crown.* 1966. London: Granada, 1978.

Sessional Papers of the House of Lords in the Session 1837–38. Vol. VIII. Accounts and Papers. 1838.

Shakespeare, Henry. *The Wild Sports of India.* London: Smith, Elder, 1862.

Shakespeare, John. 'Regarding Badheks and T'hegs', *Asiatic Researches* 13 (1820): 282–92.
Sherwood, R. 'Of the Murderers Called Phansigars', *Asiatic Researches* 13 (1820): 250–82.
Sleeman, W. H. *Ramaseeana, or, a Vocabulary of the Peculiar Language Used by the Thugs.* Calcutta: Military Orphans, 1836.
———. *Report on the Depredations Committed by the Thug Gangs of Upper and Central India.* Calcutta: O. H. Huttmann, 1840.
———. *Thugs, or Phansigars of India.* Philadelphia: Carey and Hart, 1839.
Southey, Robert. *The Curse of Kehama.* London: Longman, Hurst, Rees, Orme, and Brown, 1810.
Steel, Flora Annie. *The Garden of Fidelity: Being the Autobiography of Flora Annie Steel, 1847–1929.* London: Macmillan, 1929.
———. *On the Face of the Waters.* 1896. New Delhi: Arnold Heinemann, 1985.
———. *Voices in the Night.* London: William Heinemann, 1900.
Steel, Flora Annie and Grace Gardiner. *The Complete Indian Housekeeper and Cook.* 1888. London: William Heinemann, 1909. Revised ed.
Stevenson, J. A. R. 'Some Account of the Phansigars, or Gang-Robbers and of the Shudgarshids, or Tribes of Jugglers', *Journal of the Royal Asiatic Society* 1 (1834): 280–3.
Subramanian, Lakshmi. *Three Merchants of Bombay.* New Delhi: Penguin, 2012.
Taylor, Meadows. *Confessions of a Thug.* 1839. London: Henry S. King, 1873.
Taylor, Philip Meadows. *Seeta.* 1872. New Delhi: Asian Educational Services, 1989.
Terry, Edward. *A Voyage to East-India.* London: T. Martin and T. Allestrye, 1655.
Thompson, Edward. *Suttee: A Historical and Philosophical Inquiry.* London: George Allen, 1928.
Thornhill, Mark. *The Personal Adventures and Experiences of a Magistrate During the Rise, Progression and Suppression of the Indian Mutiny.* London: John Murray, 1884.
Thornton, Edward. *Illustrations of the history and practices of the Thugs, and notices of some of the proceedings of the government of India, for the suppression of the crime of thuggee.* London: WH Allen, 1837.
Trevelyan, G. O. *The Competition Wallah.* London: Macmillan, 1864.
———. *Cawnpore.* London: Macmillan, 1866. 3rd ed.
———. *Cawnpore.* 1865. New York: Macmillan, 1894.
Trevor, G. H. 'The Suttee of Gorah's Wife', in *Rhymes of Rajputana.* Ed. G. H. Trevor. London: Macmillan, 1894. 32–3.
Tyrwhitt, Robert Philip and Thomas William Tyndale. *A Digest of the Public General Statutes.* London: A. Strahan, 1822. Vol. 1.
Tytler, Harriet. *An Englishwoman in India: The Memoirs of Harriet Tytler 1828–1858.* Ed. Anthony Sattin. Oxford: Oxford University Press, 1986.

Valentia, Lord. [George Annesley]. *Voyages and Travels to India, Ceylon, the Red Sea, Abyssinia, and Egypt: In the Years 1802, 1803, 1804, 1805, and 1806*. London: F., C., and J. Rivington, 1811. Vol. 1.

Ward, William. *An Account of the Writings, Religion and Manners of the Hindoos*. 1818. London: Kingsbury, Parbury and Allen, 1822. Vol. 3.

Watt, George. *A Dictionary of the Economic Products of India: Vol. 2. Cabbage to Cyperus*. Cambridge: Cambridge University Press, 2014.

Webb, William Trego. *English Etiquette for Indian Gentlemen*. 1895. Calcutta: S. K. Lahiri, 1915. 5th ed.

Weston, Christine. *Indigo*. 1943. New Delhi: Indus-HarperCollins, 1993.

Wheeler, J. Talboys. *Early Records of British India: History of the English Settlements in India*. 1878. New Delhi: Asian Educational Services, 1996.

Whitworth, George Clifford. *An Anglo-Indian Dictionary*. London: Kegan Paul and Trench, 1885.

Williamson, Thomas. *The East India Vade-Mecum, or, Complete Guide to Gentlemen Intended for the Civil, Military, or Naval Service of the Hon: East India Company*. London: Black, Parry and Kingsbury, 1810. 2 vols.

———. *Oriental Field Sports; being a Complete, Detailed, and Accurate Description of the Wild Sports of the East*. With drawings by Samuel Howitt. London: H. R. Young, 1819. 2nd ed. 2 vols.

Williamson, Thomas and Charles D'Oyly. *Costumes and Customs of Modern India*. London: E. Orme, 1813.

Wilson, H. H. 'Introduction', Thomas Roebuck (compiled) *A Collection of Proberbs: And Proverbial Phrases, in the Persian and Hindoostanee Languages*. Ed. H. H. Wilson. Calcutta: Hindostanee Press, 1824.

Young, Arthur. *A Six Weeks Tour through the Southern Counties of England and Wales*. Dublin: np, 1768.

Yule, Henry and A. C. Burnell. *Hobson-Jobson: The Definitive Glossary of British India*. Selected by Kate Teltscher. Oxford: Oxford University Press, 2015.

Secondary sources

Abrams, M. H. *The Milk of Paradise: The Effect of Opium Visions on the Works of DeQuincey, Crabbe, Francis Thompson, and Coleridge*. Cambridge: Harvard University Press, 1934.

Adas, Michael. *Machines as the Measure of Men: Science, Technology, and Ideologies of Western Dominance*. Ithaca: Cornell University press, 1990.

Ahuja, Ravi. 'Mobility and Containment: The Voyages of South Asian Seamen, c.1900–1960', *ISRH* 51. Supplement (2006): 111–41.

Alavi, Seema. *Muslim Cosmopolitanism in the Age of Empire*. Cambridge: Harvard University Press, 2015.

Allen, Charles (ed). *Plain Tales from the Raj: Images of British India in the Twentieth Century*. London: Futura, 1976.

———. *Raj: A Scrapbook of British India, 1877–1947*. London: Andre Deutsch, 1977.

BIBLIOGRAPHY

———. *Soldier Sahibs: The Men Who Made the North-West Frontier*. London: Abacus, 2000.

Archer, Mildred. *Company Drawings in the India Office Library*. London: Her Majesty's Stationery Office, 1972.

Arnold, David. *Police Power and Colonial Rule: Madras 1859–1947*. New Delhi: Oxford University Press, 1986.

———. *Colonizing the Body: State Medicine and Epidemic Disease in Nineteenth-Century India*. Berkeley: University of California Press, 1993.

Balachandran, G. 'South Asian Seafarers and Their Worlds: C. 1870–1930s'. http://webdoc.sub.gwdg.de/ebook/p/2005/history_cooperative/www.historycooperative.org/proceedings/seascapes/balachandran.html. Accessed 3 March 2016.

Ballhatchet, Kenneth. *Race, Sex and Class under the Raj: Imperial Attitudes and Policies and Their Critics*. London: Weidenfeld and Nicholson, 1980.

Barr, Pat. *The Memsahibs: The Women of Victorian India*. New Delhi: Allied, 1978.

Bayly, C. A. *Imperial Meridian: The British Empire and the World, 1780–1830*. London: Longman, 1989.

———. *Empire and Information: Intelligence-Gathering and Social Communication in India*. Cambridge: Cambridge University Press, 1999.

Bhabha, Homi K. *The Location of Culture*. 1994. London: Routledge, 2009.

Blunt, Alison. 'Imperial Cartographies of Home: British Domesticity in India, 1886–1925', *Transactions of the British Institute of Geographers* 24 (1999): 421–40.

Brantlinger, Patrick. *Rule of Darkness: British Literature and Imperialism, 1830–1914*. Ithaca: Cornell University Press, 1988.

Bressey, Caroline. 'Exploring Black Women's Writing in London, 1880–1920', in *Critical Perspectives on Colonialism: Writing the Empire from Below*. Ed. Fiona Paisley and Kirsty Reid. London: Routledge, 2013. 179–98.

Cannadine, David. *Ornamentalism: How the British Saw Their Empire*. London: Penguin, 2002.

Caplan, Lionel. *Children of Colonialism: Anglo-Indians in a Postcolonial World*. Oxford: Berg, 2001.

Chakravorty, Pallabi. 'Dance, Pleasure, and Indian Women as Multisensorial Subjects', *Visual Anthropology* 17.1 (2004): 1–17.

Chattopadhyay, Swati. *Representing Calcutta: Modernity, Nationalism, and the Colonial Uncanny*. London and New York: Routledge, 2005.

———. 'The Other Face of Primitive Accumulation: The Garden House in British Colonial Bengal', in *Colonial Modernities: Building, Dwelling and Architecture in British India and Ceylon*. Ed. Peter Scriver and Vikramaditya Prakash. London: Routledge, 2007. 169–97.

Chaudhuri, K. N. *The English East India Company: The Study of an Early Joint-Stock Company 1600–1640*. London: Taylor and Francis, 1965.

Chaudhuri, Nupur. 'Memsahibs and Motherhood in Nineteenth-Century Colonial India', *Victorian Studies* 31.4 (1988): 517–35.

Cheesman, David. '"The Omnipresent Bania": Rural Moneylenders in Nineteenth-Century Sind', *Modern Asian Studies* 16:3 (1982): 445–62.

Cohen, Benjamin B. *In the Club: Associational Life in Colonial South Asia*. Hyderabad: Orient BlackSwan, 2015.

Cohn, Bernard S. *Colonialism and Its Forms of Knowledge: The British in India*. New Delhi: Oxford University Press, 1996.

Collingham, E. M. *Imperial Bodies*. London: Polity, 2001.

Collingham, Lizzie. *Curry: A Tale of Cooks and Conquerors*. Oxford: Oxford University Press, 2006.

Collis, Maurice. *Foreign Mud: The Opium Imbroglio at Canton in the 1830s and the Anglo-Chinese War*. New York: W. W. Norton, 1968.

Crook, Nigel. *The Transmission of Knowledge in South Asia: Essays on Education, Religion, History, and Politics*. New Delhi: Oxford University Press, 1996.

Dalrymple, William. *White Mughals: Love and Betrayal in Eighteenth-Century India*. New Delhi: Penguin, 2004.

Daly, Suzanne. 'Kashmir Shawls in Mid-Victorian Novels', *Victorian Literature and Culture* 30.1 (2002): 237–56.

Dash, Mike. *Thug: The True Story of India's Murderous Cult*. London: Granta, 2011.

Döring, Tobias. *Caribbean-English Passages: Intertextuality in a Postcolonial Tradition*. London: Routledge, 2003.

Dube, Saurabh. *Stitches on Time: Colonial Textures and Postcolonial Tangles*. Oxford: Oxford University Press, 2004.

Edwardes, Michael. *The Sahibs and the Lotus: The British in India*. London: Constable, 1988.

Edwards, David B. 'Mad Mullahs and Englishmen: Discourse in the Colonial Encounter', *Comparative Studies in Society and History* 31.4 (1989): 649–70.

Ernst, Waltraud. *Mad Tales from the Raj: Colonial Psychiatry in South Asia, 1800–58*. London: Anthem, 2010.

Fisher, Michael H. *Counterflows to Colonialism: Indian Travellers and Settlers in Britain, 1600–1857*. New Delhi: Permanent Black, 2004.

———. 'Working Across the Seas: Indian Maritime Labourers in India, Britain, and in between, 1600–1857', *IRSH* 51 (2006): 21–45.

Forbes, James. *Oriental Memoirs: A Narrative of Seventeen Years Residence in India*. 1813. London: Richard Bentley, 1834. 2nd ed. 4 vols.

Freitag, Sandria B. 'Collective Crime and Authority in North India', in *Crime and Criminality in British India*. Ed. Anand Yang. Tucson: University of Arizona Press, 1985. 140–56.

Friedlander, Peter. 'Hindustani Textbooks from the Raj', *Electronic Journal of Foreign Language Teaching* 3.1 (2006): 39–56.

Fulford, Tim. 'Plants, Pagodas and Penises: Southey's Oriental Imports', in *Robert Southey and the Contexts of English Romanticism*. Ed. Lynda Pratt. London: Ashgate, 2013. 187–202.

George, Rosemary Marangoly. 'Homes in the Empire, Empires in the Home', *Cultural Critique* 26 (1993–94): 95–127.

Ghosh, Kaushik. 'A Market for Aboriginality: Primitivism and Race Classification in the Indentured Labour Market of Colonial India', in *Subaltern Studies X*. Ed. Gautam Bhadra, Gyan Prakash and Susie Tharu. New Delhi: Oxford University Press, 1999. 8–48.

Gilmartin, Sophie. 'The Sati, the Bride, and the Widow: Sacrificial Woman in the Nineteenth Century', *Victorian Literature and Culture* 25.1 (1997): 141–58.

Goswami, Manu. '"Englishness" on the Imperial Circuit: Mutiny Tours in Colonial South Asia', *Journal of Historical Sociology* 9.1 (1996): 54–84.

Gough, Kathleen. 'Indian Peasant Uprisings', *Economic and Political Weekly* 9.32/34 (1974): 1391–412.

Goulding, Christopher. 'Jungle: Antedating the Entry in OED', *Notes and Queries* 53.1 (2006): 30.

Green, Nile. *Islam and the Army in Colonial India: Sepoy Religion in the Service of Empire*. Cambridge: Cambridge University Press, 2009.

Grewal, Inderpal. *Home and Harem: Nation, Gender, Empire and Cultures of Travel*. London: Leicester University Press, 1996.

Grove, Richard H. 'Colonial Conservation, Ecological Hegemony and Popular Resistance: Towards a Global Synthesis', in *Imperialism and the Natural World*. Ed. John M. McKenzie. Manchester: Manchester University Press, 1990. 15–50.

Guha, Ramachandra. 'Cricket and Politics in Colonial India', *Past & Present* 161 (1998): 155–90.

Guha, Ranajit. *Elementary Aspects of Peasant Insurgency*. New Delhi: Oxford University Press, 1983.

Hagerman, C. A. *Britain's Imperial Muse: The Classics, Imperialism, and the Indian Empire, 1784–1914*. London: Palgrave-Macmillan, 2013.

Harris, Jonathan Gil. *The First Firangis*. New Delhi: Aleph, 2015.

Harrison, Mark. *Public Health in British India: Anglo-Indian Preventive Medicine 1859–1914*. Cambridge: Cambridge University Press, 1994.

Heathcote, T. A. *The Military in British India: The Development of British Land Forces in South Asia, 1600–1947*. Manchester: Manchester University Press, 1995.

Herbert, Christopher. *War of No Pity: The Indian Mutiny and Victorian Trauma*. Princeton: Princeton University Press, 2008.

Herman, Judith. 'Men and Women of Feeling: Conventions of Sensibility and Sentimentality in the Sati Debate and Mainwaring's *The Suttee*', *Comparative Literature Studies* 42.2 (2005): 223–63.

Hibbert, Christopher. *The Great Mutiny India 1857*. London: Allen Lane, 1978.

Hosali, Priya. *Butler English: Form and Function*. Madras: B. R., 2000.

Hyam, Ronald. *Empire and Sexuality*. Manchester: Manchester University Press, 1990.

BIBLIOGRAPHY

Jacob, T. *Cantonments in India: Evolution and Growth*. New Delhi: Reliance, 1994.

James, Lawrence. *Raj: The Making and Unmaking of British India*. 1997. London: Abacus, 2003.

Jeffrey, Robin, Nandini Sundar, with Abha Mishra, Neeraj Peter, and Pradeep Tharakan. 'A Move from Minor to Major: Competing Discourses of Non-Timber Forest Products in India', in *Nature in the Global South: Environmental Projects in South and Southeast Asia*. Ed. Paul Greenough. Durham, NC: Duke University Press, 2003. 79–103.

Joseph, Betty. *Reading the East India Company, 1720–1840: Colonial Currencies of Gender*. Chicago: University of Chicago Press, 2004.

Kannabiran, Kalpana and Vasanth Kannabiran. *Muvalur Ramamirthammal's Web of Deceit: Devadasi Reform in Colonial India*. New Delhi: Kali for Women, 2003.

Keay, John. *The Honourable Company: A History of the English East India Company*. London: HarperCollins, 1993.

Kelly, John D. '"Coolie" as a Labour Commodity: Race, Sex, and European Dignity in Colonial Fiji', *Journal of Peasant Studies* 19.3–4 (1992): 246–67.

Kennedy, Dane. *The Magic Mountains: Hill Stations and the British Raj*. Berkeley: University of California Press, 1996.

King, Anthony D. *The Bungalow: The Production of a Global Culture*. Oxford: Oxford University Press, 2000. 2nd ed.

———. *Colonial Urban Development: Culture, Social Power and Environment*. London: Routledge, 2007.

Kling, Blair. *The Blue Mutiny: The Indigo Disturbances in Bengal, 1859–1962*. 1966. Calcutta: Firma K. L. M., 1977.

Krishnaswamy, Revathi. *Effeminism: The Economy of Colonial Desire*. Ann Arbor: University of Michigan Press, 1998.

Kumar, Prakash. *Indigo Plantations and Science in Colonial India*. Cambridge: Cambridge University Press, 2012.

Leask, Nigel. 'Towards an Anglo-Indian Poetry? The Colonial Muse in the Writings of John Leyden, Thomas Medwin and Charles D'Oyly', in *Writing India, 1757–1990: The Literature of British India*. Ed. Bart Moore-Gilbert. Manchester: Manchester University Press, 1996. 52–85.

Lelyveld, David. 'The Fate of Hindustani: Colonial Knowledge and the Project of a National Language', in *Orientalism and the Postcolonial Predicament: Perspectives on South Asia*. Ed. Carol Breckenridge and Peter van der Veer. University of Pennsylvania Press, 1993. 189–214.

Lester, Alan. 'Obtaining the "Due Observance of Justice": The Geographies of Global Humanitarianism', *Environment and Planning D* 20.3 (2000): 277–93.

———. 'Humanism, Race and the Colonial Frontier', *Transactions of British Geographers*, New Series, 37 (2012): 132–48.

Levine, Philippa. *Prostitution, Race, and Politics: Policing Venereal Disease in the British Empire*. Durham, NC: Duke University Press, 2003.

―――. 'Introduction: Why Gender and Empire?', in *Gender and Empire*. Ed. Levine, Philippa. Oxford: Oxford University Press, 2004. 1–13.

Macfie, A. L. 'Thuggee: An Orientalist Construction?', *Rethinking History* 12 (2008): 383–97.

MacKenzie, J. M. 'The Imperial Pioneer and Hunter and the British Masculine Stereotype in Late Victorian and Edwardian Times', in *Manliness and Morality: Masculinity in Britain and America 1800–1940*. Ed. J. A. Mangan and J. Walvin. New York: St. Martin's, 1987. 176–98.

―――. *The Empire of Nature: Hunting, Conservation and British Imperialism*. Manchester: Manchester University Press, 1988.

Macmillan, Margaret. *Women of the Raj*. London: Thames and Hudson, 1988.

Mahmud, Tayyab. 'Cheaper Than a Slave: Indentured Labor, Colonialism and Capitalism', *Whittier Law Review* 34.215 (2013). http://digitalcommons.law.seattleu.edu/cgi/viewcontent.cgi?article=1139&context=faculty

Majumdar, Boria. *Cricket in Colonial India 1780–1947*. London: Routledge, 2013.

Mangan, J. A. (ed). *The Cultural Bond: Sport, Empire, Society*. London: Frank Cass, 1992.

Mani, Lata. *Contentious Traditions: The Debate on Sati in Colonial India*. Berkeley: University of California Press, 1998.

Mason, Philip. *The Men Who Ruled India*. London: Pan, 1987.

Matar, Nabil. *Turks, Moors and Englishmen in the Age of Discovery*. New York: Columbia University Press, 2000.

McDevitt, Patrick. *May the Best Man Win: Sport, Masculinity and Nationalism in Great Britain and the Empire, 1880–1935*. London: Palgrave-Macmillan, 2004.

McKenzie, C. 'The British Big-Game Hunting Tradition, Masculinity and Fraternalism with Particular Reference to the "Shikar-Club"', *The Sport Historian* 20.1 (2000): 70–96.

Miller, Jan and Gregory Stanczak. 'Redeeming, Ruling, and Reaping: British Missionary Societies, the East India Company, and the India-to-China Opium Trade', *Journal for the Scientific Study of Religion* 48.2 (2009): 332–52.

Milligan, Barry. *Pleasures and Pains: Opium and the Orient in Nineteenth-Century British Culture*. Charlottesville and London: University press of Virginia, 1995.

Mir, Farina. *The Social Space of Language: Vernacular Culture in British Colonial Punjab*. Berkeley and London: University of California Press, 2010.

Mishra, Vijay. *The Literature of the Indian Diaspora: Theorizing the Diasporic Imaginary*. London: Routledge, 2007.

Mukherjee, Pablo. 'Nimrods: Hunting, Authority, Identity', *Modern Language Review* 100.4 (2005): 923–39.

Mukherjee, Rudransghu. *Awadh in Revolt, 1857–1858: A Study of Popular Resistance*. Hyderabad: Orient BlackSwan, 2002.

Mundy, Peter. *The Travls of Peter Mundy in Europe and Asia, 1608–1667*. Cambridge: The Hakluyt Society, Vol. 2 (1907): 354–5.

Nair, Janaki. *Women and Law in Colonial India: A Social History*. New Delhi: Kali for Women, 1996.

Nayar, Pramod K. *English Writing and India, 1600–1920: Colonizing Aesthetics*. London: Routledge, 2008.

———. *Colonial Voices: The Discourses of Empire*. Malden, MA: Wiley-Blackwell, 2012.

———. 'The "Disorderly Memsahib": Political Domesticity in Alice Perrin's Empire Fiction', *Brno Studies in English* 38.1 (2012): 123–38.

———. 'Civil Modernity: The Management of Manners and Polite Imperial Relations in India, 1880–1930', *South Asia* (forthcoming).

Nechtman, Tillman W. *Nabobs: Empire and Identity in Eighteenth-Century Britain*. Cambridge: Cambridge University Press, 2010.

Niranjana, Tejaswini. *Siting Translation: History, Post-Structuralism and the Colonial Context*. Hyderabad: Orient BlackSwan, 1995.

Northrup, David. *Indentured Labor in the Age of Imperialism, 1834–1922*. Cambridge: Cambridge University Press, 1995.

O'Connor, Daniel. *Chaplains of the East India Company, 1601–1858*. London: A & C Black, 2012.

Ogborn, Miles. *Indian Ink: Script and Print in the Making of the English East India Company*. Chicago and London: Chicago University Press, 2007.

Orr, Leslie C. *Donors, Devotees, and Daughters of God: Temple Women in Medieval Tamilnadu*. New York: Oxford University Press, 2000.

Palsetia, Jesse S. 'The Parsis of India and the Opium Trade in China', *Contemporary Drug Problems* 35 (2008): 647–78.

Pandian, A. S. 'Predatory Care: The Imperial Hunt in Mughal and British India', *Journal of Historical Sociology* 14.1 (2001): 79–107.

Parkes, Peter. 'Indigenous Polo in Northern Pakistan: Game and Power on the Periphery', in *Subaltern Sports: Politics and Sport in South Asia*. Ed. James H. Mills. London: Anthem, 2005. 61–82.

Parry, Benita. *Delusions and Discoveries*. London: Verso, 1998.

Patterson, Steven. *The Cult of Imperial Honor in British India*. London: Palgrave Macmillan, 2009.

Paxton, Nancy L. *Writing Under the Raj: Gender, Race and Rape in the British Colonial Imagination, 1830–1947*. London: Rutgers University Press, 1999.

Peers, Douglas, 'Imperial Vice', in *Guardians of Empire: The Armed Forces of the Colonial Powers, C. 1700–1964*. Ed. David Killingray and David Omissi. Manchester: Manchester University Press, 1999. 25–52.

Pinch, W. R. *Warrior Ascetics and Indian Empires*. Cambridge: Cambridge University Press, 2006.

Porter, David. 'Chinoiserie and the Aesthetics of Illegitimacy', *Studies in Eighteenth-Century Culture* 28 (1999): 27–54.

———. 'Monstrous Beauty: Eighteenth-Century Fashion and the Aesthetics of the Chinese Taste', *Eighteenth-Century Studies* 35.3 (2002): 395–411.

Raj, Kapil. 'Refashioning Civilities, Engineering Trust: William Jones, Indian Intermediaries and the Production of Reliable Legal Knowledge in Late Eighteenth-Century Bengal', *Studies in History*, ns, 17.2 (2001): 175–209.

Raman, Bhavani. *Document Raj: Writing and Scribes in Early Colonial South India*. Chicago and London: University of Chicago Press, 2012.

Richards, John F. 'Opium and the British Indian Empire: The Royal Commission of 1895', *Modern Asian Studies* 36.2 (2002): 375–420.

Robins, Nick. *The Corporation That Changed the World: How the East India Company Shaped the Modern Multinational*. Hyderabad: Orient Longman, 2006.

Roy, Anindyo. *Civility and Empire: Literature and Culture in British India 1822–1922*. London: Routledge, 2005.

Roy, Parama. *Indian Traffic: Identities in Question in Colonial and Postcolonial India*. New Delhi: Vistaar, 1998.

Roy, Tirthankar. 'Indigo and Law in Colonial India', *Economic History Review* 64.S1 (2011): 60–75.

Scott, Paul. *The Jewel in the Crown*. 1966. London: Granada, 1978.

Sen, Indrani. 'Colonial Domesticities, Contentious Interactions: Ayahs, Wet-Nurses and Memsahibs in Colonial India', *Indian Journal of Gender Studies* 16.3 (2009): 299–328.

———. 'Devoted Wife/Sensuous Bibi: Colonial Constructions of the Indian Woman, 1860–1900', *Indian Journal of Gender Studies* 8.1 (2001).

———. *Women and Empire: Representations in the Writings of British India (1858–1900)*. Hyderabad: Orient Longman, 2002.

———. 'Discourses of "Gendered Loyalty": Indian Women in Nineteenth-Century Mutiny Fiction', in *The Great Rebellion of 1857 in India: Exploring Transgressions, Contests and Diversities*. Ed. Biswamoy Pati. London: Routledge, 2010. 1–22.

Sharpe, Jenny. *Allegories of Empire: The Figure of the Woman in the Colonial Text*. Minneapolis: University of Minnesota Press, 1993.

Siebenga, Rianne. 'Colonial India's "Fanatical Fakirs" and their Popular Representations', *History and Anthropology* 23.4 (2012): 445–6.

Singer, Katherine. 'Stoned Shelley: Revolutionary Tactics and Women under the Influence', *Studies in Romanticism* 48.4 (2009): 687–707.

Singh, Gajendra. *The Testimonies of Indian Soldiers and the Two World Wars: Between Self and Sepoy*. London: Bloomsbury, 2014.

Singha, Radhika. *A Despotism of Law: Crime and Justice in Early Colonial India*. 1998. New Delhi: Oxford University Press, 2000.

Sinha, Mrinalini. *Colonial Masculinity: The 'Manly Englishman' and the 'Effeminate Bengali' in the Nineteenth Century*. Manchester: Manchester University Press, 1995.

———. 'Britishness, Clubbability, and the Colonial Public Sphere: The Genealogy of an Imperial Institution in Colonial India', *Journal of British Studies* 40 (2001): 489–521.

BIBLIOGRAPHY

Snape, Michael. *The Royal Army Chaplains Department: Clergy under Fire.* Martlesham, Suffolk: Boydell and Brewer, 2007.

Soneji, Davesh. *Unfinished Gestures: Devadasis, Memory, and Modernity in South India.* Chicago and London: University of Chicago Press, 2012.

Spear, Percival. *The Nabobs: A Study of the Social Life of the English in Eighteenth Century India.* Oxford: Curzon, 1963.

Spivak, Gayatri Chakravorty. 'How to Read a "Culturally Different" Book', in *Colonial Discourse/Postcolonial Theory.* Ed. Francis Barker, Peter Hulme, and Margeret Iverson. Manchester: Manchester University Press, 1996. 126–50.

Srinivasan, Amrit. 'Reform and Revival: The Devadasi and Her Dance', *Economic and Political Weekly* 20.44 (1985): 1869–76.

Starke, Ulrike. *An Empire of Books: The Naval Kishore Press and the Diffusion of the Printed Word in Colonial India.* Ranikhet: Permanent Black, 2009.

Steadman-Jones, Richard. *Colonialism and Grammatical Representation: John Gilchrist and the Analysis of the 'Hindustani' Language in the Late Eighteenth and Early Nineteenth Centuries.* Oxford: Blackwell, 2007.

Stoler, Ann Laura. 'Rethinking Colonial Categories: European Communities and the Boundaries of Rule', *Comparative Studies in Society and History* 31 (1989): 134–61.

Sundström, Lars. *The Exchange Economy of Pre-Colonial Tropical Africa.* London: C. Hurst, 1974.

Tambe, Ashwini. *Codes of Conduct: Regulating Prostitution in Late Colonial Bombay.* Minneapolis and London: University of Minnesota Press, 2009.

Teltscher, Kate. 'Introduction', in *Hobson-Jobson: The Definitive Glossary of British India.* Ed. Henry Yule and A. C. Burnell. Oxford: Oxford University Press, 2015. xi–xxxix.

Tickell, Alex. 'Cawnpore, Kipling and Charivari: 1857 and the Politics of Commemoration', *Literature and History* 18.2 (2009): 1–19.

Valentini, AL. *Lascari-Bat: A Collection of Sentences Used in the Daily Routine of a Modern Passenger Ship.* London: Miller & Sons, 1892.

Van Woerkens, M. *The Strangled Traveller: Colonial Imaginings and the Thugs of India.* Chicago: Chicago University Press, 2002.

Vasunia, Phiroze. *The Classics and Colonial India.* London: Oxford University Press, 2013.

Vaughan, Alden T. and Virginia Mason Vaughan. 'Before Othello: Elizabethan Representations of Sub-Saharan Africans', *The William and Mary Quarterly*, Third Series, 54.1 (1997): 19–44.

Visram, Rozina. *Ayahs, Lascars and Princes: Indians in Britain 1700–1947.* London: Macmillan, 1986.

———. *Asians in Britain: 400 Years of History.* London: Pluto, 2002.

Wagner, Kim A. 'The Deconstructed Stranglers: A Reassessment of Thuggee', *Modern Asian Studies* 38 (2004): 931–63.

———. *The Great Fear of 1857: Rumours, Conspiracies and the Making of the Indian Uprising.* Oxford: Peter Lang, 2010.

Wald, Erica. 'Health, Discipline and Appropriate Behaviour: The Body of the Soldier and Space of the Cantonment', *Modern Asian Studies* 46 (2012): 815–56.

———. *Vice in the Barracks: Medicine, the Military and the Making of Colonial India, 1780–1868*. London: Palgrave-Macmillan, 2014.

Ward, Andrew. *Our Bones Are Scattered: The Cawnpore Massacres and the Indian Mutiny of 1857*. London: John Murray, 2004.

Ware, Vron. *Beyond the Pale: White Women, Racism and History*. London: Verso, 1992.

Wilson, A. N. *The Victorians*. London: Random House, 2011.

Yang, Anand A. *Bazaar India: Markets, Society, and the Colonial State in Bihar*. Berkeley: University of California Press, 1999.

Yegenoglu, Meyda. *Colonial Fantasies: Towards a Feminist Reading of Orientalism*. Cambridge: Cambridge University Press, 1998.

Zutshi, Chitralekha. 'Designed for Eternity: Kashmiri Shawls, Empire, and Cultures of Production and Consumption in Mid-Victorian Britain', *Journal of British Studies* 48.2 (2009): 420–40.